THE ESSENTIAL BOOK
OF CROCHET
TECHNIQUES

Nancie M. Wiseman

Martingale®
& COMPANY

The Essential Book
of Crochet Techniques
© 2006 by Nancie M. Wiseman

Martingale & Company
20205 144th Avenue NE
Woodinville, WA 98072-8478 USA
www.martingale-pub.com

Printed in China
11 10 09 08 07 06   8 7 6 5 4 3 2 1

All garments shown are from *Classic Crocheted Vests* by Nancie M. Wiseman (Martingale & Company, 2004).

Library of Congress Cataloging-in-Publication Data
Wiseman, Nancie M.
   The essential book of crochet techniques / Nancie M. Wiseman.
      p. cm.
   Includes index.
   ISBN 1-56477-629-8
   1. Crocheting—patterns. I. Title.
   TT820.W6165 2006
   746.43'4—dc22
                              2005018340

Mission Statement

Dedicated to providing quality products and service to inspire creativity.

Credits

President: Nancy J. Martin
CEO: Daniel J. Martin
VP and General Manager:
   Tom Wierzbicki
Publisher: Jane Hamada
Editorial Director: Mary V. Green
Managing Editor: Tina Cook
Technical Editor: Ursula Reikes
Copy Editor: Liz McGehee
Design Director: Stan Green
Illustrator: Laurel Strand
Cover and Text Designer:
   Regina Girard
Photographer: Brent Kane

Dedication

To my dear husband, Bill,
the love of my life—
need I say more?

Acknowledgments

I always feel I can never say thank you enough to the special people who help me while I'm writing a book. Everyone is so wonderful at Martingale & Company that I just can't say enough about them. Thanks to all of you for your time and patience to make my books beautiful, easy to read, and a joy to work on. A very special thanks to Ursula Reikes, my technical editor at Martingale, who has also become a dear friend. I couldn't do a book without you—thank you so much for your time and expertise.

And to Cascade Yarns, for providing the Cascade 220 that was used for all of the samples in this book. Thanks for your generosity.

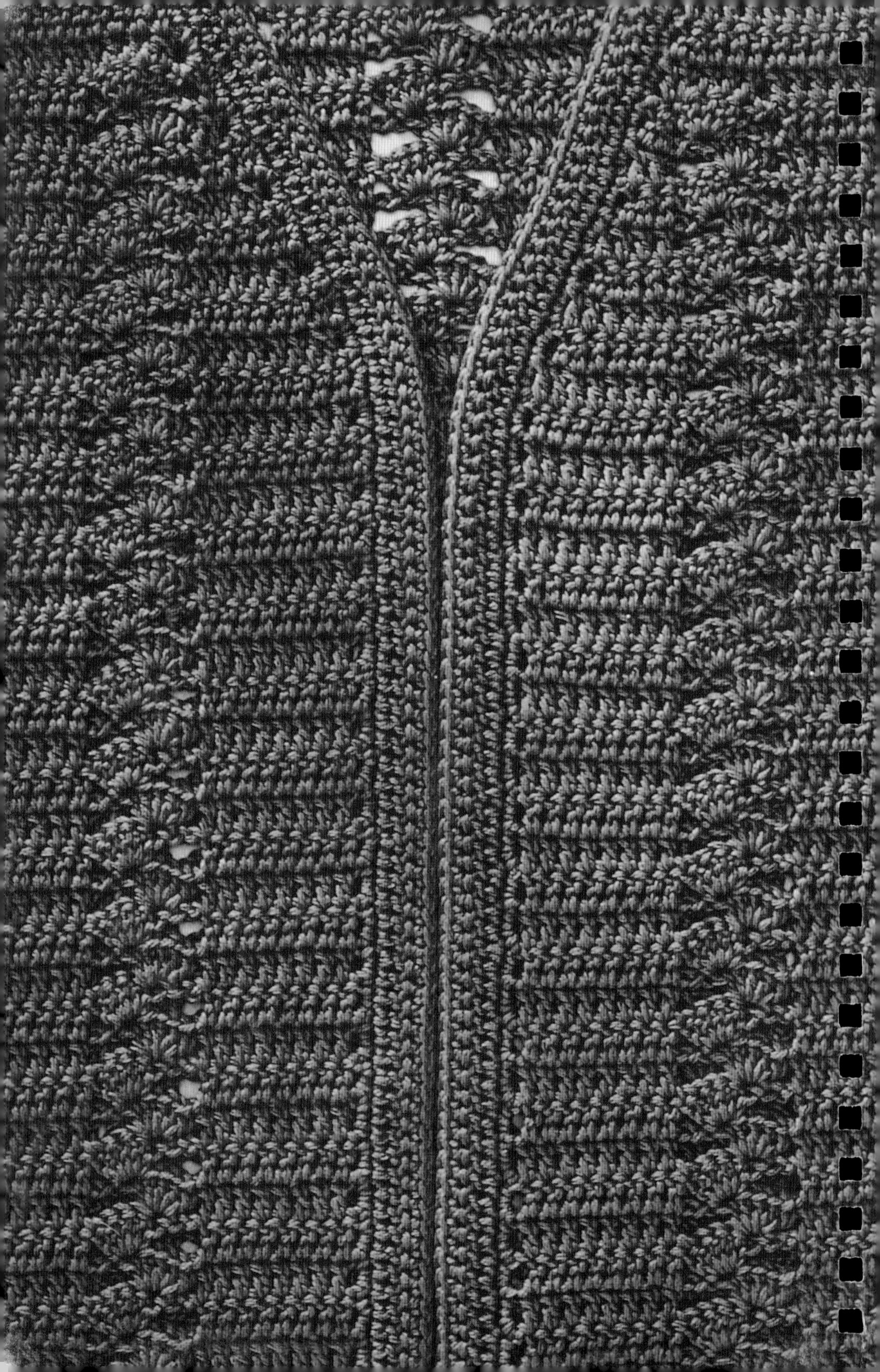

Contents

Introduction

In the United States, crochet became popular in the early 1800s and was practiced by women in all walks of life. Pioneer women traveling across the country crocheted out of necessity, making shawls, mufflers, underwear, and petticoats to help keep the family warm. Women who had more time and money crocheted for the joy of making something beautiful with their own hands. They crocheted decorative items for the home, such as doilies, lace edgings around handkerchiefs and pillowcases, as well as fanciful lace hats and gloves. During World War II, women in the service crocheted covers for their dog tags because the metal tags were cold against the skin. Through good times and bad, the Depression and war, and now into the twenty-first century, we still crochet out of need and for sheer pleasure, while aspiring to make each project more perfect than the last.

This book provides you with tools to make your projects perfect. You'll find everything from getting started with crochet to finishing your project. Included are instructions for basic stitches, a guide to reading patterns, and explanations of the symbols used to identify and categorize yarns and hooks.

My goal has been to make this the only resource you'll need to carry with you as you crochet. There are lots of photos and illustrations that will help you work stitches and finish garments with confidence. You'll find tricks and hints for making crochet easier and the results more pleasing. Plus, I've included instructions for three of my favorite techniques: filet crochet, intarsia, and afghan stitch.

Crochet is *hot!* Don't be left out. You'll be amazed at all the wonderful things you can make. And if you're a knitter, you, too, will love using crochet for trims and borders on your knitted sweaters and afghans.

Craft Yarn Council of America Standards for Crochet

The Craft Yarn Council of America, which is made up of yarn companies, pattern manufacturers, hook and needle manufacturers, magazines, book publishers, and needlework organizations, has developed a set of standards and identifying symbols for crochet hooks, yarn weights, and skill levels. All of this is meant to make buying yarn and choosing hooks and needles easier because it makes all labeling consistent on everything you buy to work a crochet project. In this chapter, we'll outline the different standards and labels.

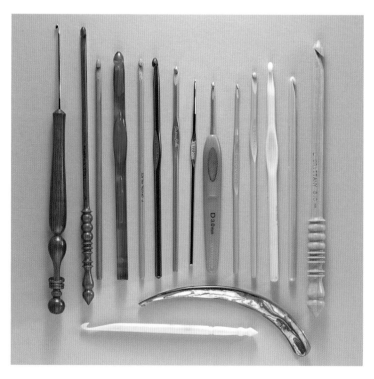

A sample of crochet hooks made in a variety of styles and from an assortment of materials

CROCHET HOOKS

Crochet hooks are labeled by size, either in millimeters (the actual size of the hook) or with letter and/or number labels (the system used by manufacturers in the United States). Below are abbreviated lists showing the most common sizes of crochet hooks and their metric and U.S. equivalents.

Plastic, Wooden, or Metal Hooks (used to work with yarn)		Steel Hooks (used to work with thread)	
Millimeter Range	U.S. Size Range*	Millimeter Range	U.S. Size Range*
2.25	B-1	3.50	00
2.75	C-2	3.25	0
3.25	D-3	2.75	1
3.5	E-4	2.25	2
3.75	F-5	2.10	3
4	G-6	2.00	4
4.5	7	1.90	5
5	H-8	1.80	6
5.5	I-9	1.65	7
6	J-10	1.50	8
6.5	K-10½		
8	L-11		
9	M/N-13		
10	N/P-15		
15	P/Q		

The millimeter size is the most accurate for sizing the hooks. The letter or number on the U.S. sizes may vary from manufacturer to manufacturer.

SKILL LEVEL

You'll find the following icons, which indicate skill level, on most patterns. Use the icons to find patterns appropriate for your ability.

Beginner

Projects that use only basic stitches. Minimal shaping.

Easy

Projects that use yarn or thread with basic stitches, repetitive stitch patterns, simple color changes, shaping, and finishing.

Intermediate

Projects that use a variety of techniques, such as basic lace patterns or color patterns, midlevel shaping, and finishing.

Experienced

Projects with intricate stitch patterns, techniques, and dimension, such as nonrepeating patterns, multicolor techniques, detailed shaping, refined finishing, and use of fine threads and small hooks.

YARN WEIGHTS

Most yarn is now labeled with a number from 1 to 6 to help you choose the right yarn for your project. This number will tell you the weight of the yarn. You can refer to the chart below to find out what hook size is appropriate for the yarn and the approximate gauge you should be getting on the hook it tells you to use. This information will help you make the right yarn choices when you need to substitute a yarn.

Yarn-Weight Symbol and Category Names	1 SUPER FINE	2 FINE	3 LIGHT	4 MEDIUM	5 BULKY	6 SUPER BULKY
Types of Yarns in Category	Sock, Fingering, Baby	Sport, Baby	DK, Light Worsted	Worsted, Afghan, Aran	Chunky, Craft, Rug	Bulky, Roving
Crochet Gauge Ranges in Single Crochet to 4"	21 to 32 sts	16 to 20 sts	12 to 17 sts	11 to 14 sts	8 to 11 sts	5 to 9 sts
Recommended Hook in Metric-Size Range	2.25 to 3.5 mm	3.5 to 4.5 mm	4.5 to 5.5 mm	5.5 to 6.5 mm	6.5 to 9 mm	9 mm and larger
Recommended Hook in U.S.-Size Range	B-1 to E-4	E-4 to 7	7 to I-9	I-9 to K-10½	K-10½ to M/N-13	M/N-13 and larger

Crochet Basics

The information in this section will get you started with crochet and provide you with a wealth of tips and hints to help you with your projects. If you crochet left-handed, it may be helpful to prop up the book in front of a mirror to view the illustrations.

SLIPKNOT

All crochet stitches begin with a slipknot. This is a loop on the hook secured with a knot at the base.

TO WORK:
Create a loop near the tail end of the yarn. From the ball end of the yarn, pull a loop through the first loop. Place the new loop on the hook, pull the yarn ends, and tighten the slipknot.

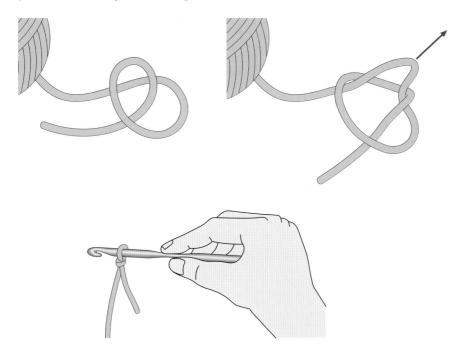

YARN OVER HOOK (YO)

To make a new stitch, you must bring the yarn over the hook and then pull it through the stitch or an existing loop on the hook. This will happen in every stitch you make.

TO WORK:
Bring the yarn from the back of the hook and lay it across the hook from back to front. The hook should do the work; don't wrap the yarn around the hook, since this will create uneven tension.

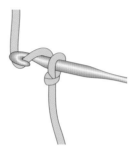

CHAIN STITCH (ch)

The chain stitch is used as the beginning for all crochet.

TO WORK:
To make a chain, start with a slipknot on the hook, yarn over hook, and pull it through the slipknot. *Yarn over hook and pull it through the loop on the hook.* Repeat from * to * for the desired number of chains. The loop on the hook does not count as a stitch.

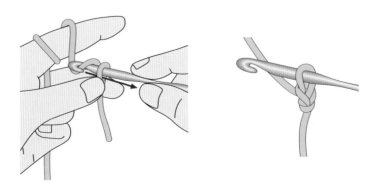

To count the number of chains, look at the front of the chain and start with the first chain at the base of the hook, that is, chain number 1. Count down the chain from there; the slipknot at the end of the chain does not count. If you're making a large chain—for example, for an afghan—it's easy to miscount the chains. To make counting easier, place a pin or marker every 20 to 25 stitches so that you don't have to recount these stitches later.

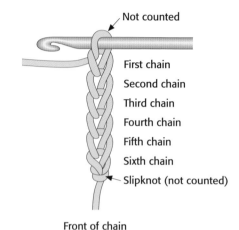

Not counted
First chain
Second chain
Third chain
Fourth chain
Fifth chain
Sixth chain
Slipknot (not counted)

Front of chain

Back of chain

Where to Insert the Hook in a Row of Chain Stitches

After the first row of chain stitches has been made and you have turned to make the next row, generally you insert the hook under the 2 top loops or V of the right side of the chain, leaving a single thread edge.

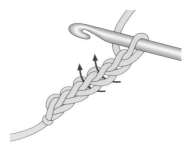

An alternative to working under both loops is to work under the top loop of the chain.

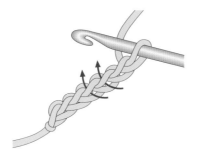

A pattern may also direct you to insert the hook through the back loop only, which will leave the 2 loops of the right side of the chain at the bottom. This edge will be a mirror image of the top edge when you're finished.

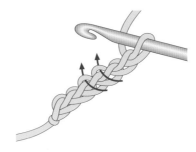

Where to Insert the Hook with Work in Progress

There are 3 areas of a stitch into which you can insert the hook. The default position is always under both threads or loops of the stitch. The second option is under the front loop (fl). The third option is under the back loop (bl). The pattern will indicate what area of the stitch to use. If the area of the stitch isn't specified, use both loops.

TO WORK:

Insert the hook into the specified area of stitch and work the designated stitch.

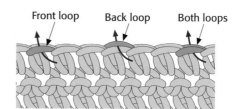

Front loop   Back loop   Both loops

SLIP STITCH (sl st)

+ A slip stitch is used to travel across stitches that you won't be using again. For example, you can use a slip stitch when shaping armholes and necks.

+ It can also be used for seams.

+ It does not add height to the work.

+ There is no turning chain.

TO WORK:

Insert the hook into the designated stitch, yarn over hook, and pull the loop through the stitch and the loop on the hook. There should be 1 loop left on the hook.

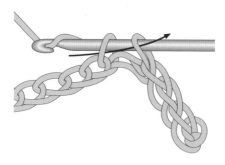

SINGLE CROCHET (sc)

The single crochet is the shortest of the 3 basic stitches, and it's a firm and tight stitch.

Between the lines of red thread are 2 rows of single crochet. The first row is worked from the right side and the second is worked from the wrong side.

+ The edges of a single crochet piece will roll.

+ It has very little stretch; it's good for warmth.

+ The height and width of 1 single crochet should be equal to 1 chain.

+ It uses 1 chain for the turning chain.

TO WORK INTO A CHAIN:

Insert the hook into the second chain from the hook, *yarn over hook, and pull through the chain (2 loops on hook).

Yarn over hook and pull through the 2 loops on the hook (1 loop remains on hook).

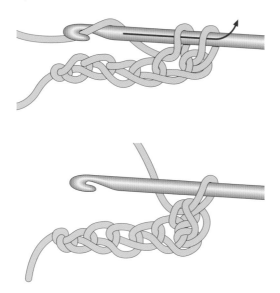

TO WORK INTO ANOTHER STITCH:

Insert the hook into the designated part of the stitch (front loop, back loop, or both loops); work from * on page 17.

HALF DOUBLE CROCHET (hdc)

A half double crochet is a half stitch taller than single crochet, and it creates a soft stitch.

Between the lines of red thread are 2 rows of half double crochet. The first row is worked from the right side and the second is worked from the wrong side.

✦ The edges of a half double crochet piece will roll slightly but less than those in single crochet.

✦ This stitch is good for warmth, but it isn't as dense as single crochet.

✦ It uses 2 chains for the turning chain (see page 26).

TO WORK INTO A CHAIN:

Yarn over hook, insert the hook into the third chain from the hook, *and pull through the chain (3 loops on hook).

Yarn over hook and pull through all 3 loops on the hook (1 loop remains on hook).

TO WORK INTO ANOTHER STITCH:
Yarn over hook, insert the hook into the designated part of the stitch (front loop, back loop, or both loops); work from * on page 19.

DOUBLE CROCHET (dc)

Double crochet is a half stitch taller than half double crochet. It's softer and more pliable than single and half double crochet stitches.

Between the lines of red thread are 2 rows of double crochet. The first row is worked from the right side and the second is worked from the wrong side.

+ The edges of a double crochet piece won't roll.

+ There are vertical spaces between the stitches that are more visible than with the single or half double crochet stitches.

+ The resulting fabric is quite durable but not heavy.

+ It uses 2 or 3 chains for the turning chain (see page 26).

TO WORK INTO A CHAIN:

Yarn over hook, insert the hook into the third or fourth chain from the hook, depending on whether you used 2 or 3 stitches for the turning chain. The illustration shows inserting the hook in the fourth chain from the hook.

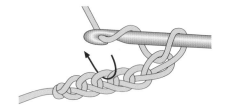

*Yarn over hook and pull through the chain (3 loops on hook). Yarn over hook and pull through 2 loops on the hook (2 loops on hook).

Yarn over hook and pull through the remaining 2 loops on the hook (1 loop remains on hook).

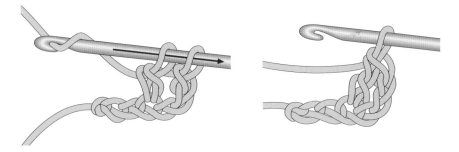

TO WORK INTO ANOTHER STITCH:

Yarn over hook, insert the hook into the designated part of the stitch (front loop, back loop, or both loops), and work from * above.

TREBLE CROCHET

Treble crochet is a half stitch taller than double crochet. It is a very soft stitch with gaps between the stitches that resemble lace.

Between the lines of red thread are 2 rows of treble crochet. The first row is worked from the right side and the second is worked from the wrong side.

✦ The edges of a treble crochet piece won't roll.

✦ The resulting fabric is delicate, and care must be taken because it will snag easily.

✦ It uses 3 or 4 stitches for a turning chain (see page 26).

✦ Work the initial chain loosely.

TO WORK INTO A CHAIN:
Yarn over hook twice, insert the hook into the fourth or fifth chain from the hook, depending on whether you use 3 or 4 stitches for the turning chain. The illustration shows going into the fifth chain from the hook.

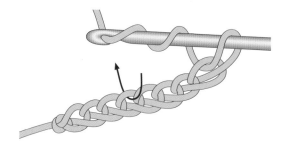

*Yarn over hook and pull through the chain stitch (4 loops on hook). Yarn over hook and pull through 2 loops on the hook (3 loops on hook).

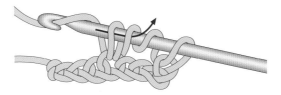

Yarn over hook and pull through 2 loops on the hook (2 loops on hook).

Yarn over hook and pull through the remaining 2 loops on the hook (1 loop remains on hook).

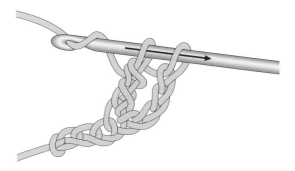

TO WORK INTO ANOTHER STITCH:
Yarn over hook twice, insert the hook into the designated part of the stitch (front loop, back loop, or both loops), and work from * above.

FRONT-POST AND BACK-POST DOUBLE CROCHET (FPdc and BPdc)

A post is the vertical part of a stitch. Working around the post of double crochet stitches in the previous row will create texture in your work. These stitches can be made around the front or back of any stitch.

Front-post double crochet in the middle of the sample

Back-post double crochet in the middle of the sample

Front-post and back-post double crochet worked together in the same piece can create a wonderful checkerboard pattern.

TO WORK FRONT-POST DOUBLE CROCHET:

Yarn over hook, insert the hook from the front around the post of a double crochet from the row below, come around the post and bring the hook out on the left side, yarn over hook and pull up a loop (3 loops on hook), yarn over hook and pull through 2 loops on the hook (2 loops on hook), yarn over hook and pull through the remaining 2 loops on the hook (1 loop remains on hook).

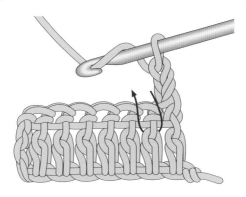

TO WORK BACK-POST DOUBLE CROCHET:

Yarn over hook, insert the hook from the back around the post of a double crochet from the row below, come around the post and twist the hook out toward the back on the left side, yarn over hook and pull through a loop, yarn over hook and pull through 2 loops on hook (2 loops on hook), yarn over hook and pull through the remaining 2 loops on the hook.

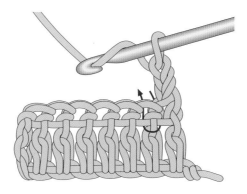

THE TURNING CHAIN (tch)

There are a variety of stitches used in crochet, but they all start out with a foundation of chain stitches. The number of chain stitches will vary, depending on what stitch you're going to work on top of the chain.

Each basic stitch adds slightly more height to the work, which becomes taller as you progress through the stitches. So every time you start a new row, the hook must be brought up to the proper level by making chain stitches that equal the height of the stitch.

Here enters what we call a "turning chain." This chain counts as a stitch (except in single crochet, where it does not count) and also matches the height of the stitch you're working. Here is an illustration showing the number of chains used for each stitch. Two chains are used for half double crochet, while double crochet can use 2 or 3 chains in the turning chain, depending on the pattern. Treble crochet can use 3 or 4 chains in the turning chain. The pattern directions will tell you how many chains to make in a turning chain for each stitch.

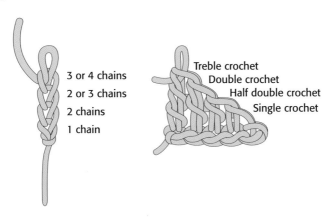

3 or 4 chains
2 or 3 chains
2 chains
1 chain

Treble crochet
Double crochet
Half double crochet
Single crochet

Turning Chains at the Start of a Project

How many chains to use in a turning chain and when the turning chain counts as a stitch is the source of much confusion. To clarify this, I recommend that you work through each of the swatches on pages 27 and 28 to fully understand how the turning chain works. For each basic stitch, we are going to make a swatch that ends up to be 10 stitches. The number of chains you need to make to end up with 10 stitches varies, as explained on pages 27 and 28.

SINGLE CROCHET:

Chain 11 stitches, single crochet in the second chain from the hook and in each chain across. The chain you skipped at the beginning does not count, so you're left with 10 stitches. Single crochet is slightly different than the rest, since the turning chain doesn't count. This is what it looks like at the beginning and end of the row.

First single crochet in row

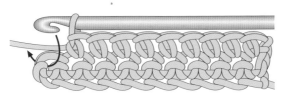

Last single crochet in row

HALF DOUBLE CROCHET:

Chain 11 stitches, half double crochet in the third chain from the hook and in each chain across. Now, you chained the same number of stitches as for single crochet and skipped 2 chains when you put the hook in, so how did you get 10 stitches? The 2 stitches you skipped become a turning chain and now count as one of the half double crochet stitches. Then you made the first half double crochet in stitch 3 from the hook, giving you 2 stitches; you now have 8 more chains in which to place a stitch, giving you a total of 10 half double crochets.

DOUBLE CROCHET:

Chain 12 stitches, double crochet in the fourth chain from the hook and in each chain across; we are using a turning chain of 3 stitches. Again, this will seem odd, but the same explanation works as for half double crochet. The 3 stitches you skipped count as 1 stitch, plus the double crochet you made makes 2 stitches, and once again you have 8 chains in which to place a stitch, giving you a total of 10 double crochets. If you use 2 chains for the turning chain, you will chain 11 stitches and double crochet in the third chain from the hook.

TREBLE CROCHET:

Chain 13 stitches, treble crochet in the fifth chain from the hook and in each chain across; we are using a turning chain of 4 stitches. The 4 stitches you skipped count as 1 stitch, plus the treble crochet you made makes 2 stitches. Once again you have 8 chains in which to place a stitch, giving you a total of 10 treble crochets. If you use 3 chains for the turning chain, you will chain 12 stitches and treble crochet in the fourth chain from the hook.

> ***Always use*** the number of stitches for the turning chain the pattern uses so that you don't throw the pattern off. That number will include the number of chains the directions tell you to skip before making the first stitch on the first row. Of course, this may change if the stitch pattern changes throughout the pattern.

Turning Chains at the End of a Row

What to do at the end of a row is another source of confusion if there is a turning chain at the beginning of the previous row. Not knowing where to make the first stitch and where to make the last stitch to keep the pattern intact often leads to errors.

Work the turning chain within the main body of stitches by placing the first stitch in the very next stitch after the stitch the turning chain is coming out of and by placing the last stitch in the turning chain. The turning chain will always count as the stitch it is replacing on the next row. Don't skip it; it counts as the last stitch of the next row. Most patterns will tell you where to place the last stitch. The chart below (see "Chart Instructions" on page 35) shows the turning chains within the body of work.

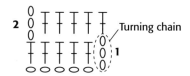

**Turning chains worked within
the body of the work**

JOINING YARN

At some point, you'll run out of yarn while working on your project. It's best to begin new yarn at a side seam but sometimes this option isn't available.

Joining at a Side Seam

To attach new yarn at the side seam, drop the old yarn and work the turning chain in the new yarn. Gently pull the tail of the new yarn to secure the join. Weave in the end now or when the project is completed.

Joining in the Middle of a Row

There are 3 methods for joining a new ball of yarn in the middle of your work. Please, never tie knots in the middle of your work because they may show on the right side of the work, or they may come untied. Besides, they aren't necessary if you use one of these methods.

METHOD 1:

Insert the hook into the appropriate stitch, work the stitch until there are 2 loops on the hook, yarn over hook with the new yarn, and pull through both loops. Proceed in the stitch pattern with the new yarn. Weave in the ends now or when the project is completed.

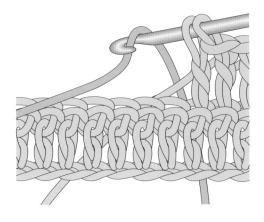

METHOD 2:

Complete the last stitch before the new yarn is needed. Drop the old yarn, yarn over, pull the new yarn through, and pull down snugly on the tails of the new and old yarn. Weave in the ends now or when the project is completed.

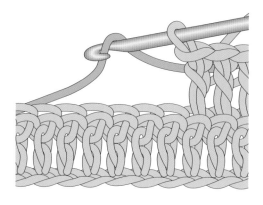

METHOD 3:

Work to 5 stitches in advance of changing to the new yarn. Lay the new yarn over the unworked stitches, and crochet 4 stitches over the new yarn as follows (the example below is done in single crochet, but this will work with any stitch):

　*Insert the hook into the next stitch and under the new yarn, yarn over hook, pull a loop through, yarn over hook, and pull through both loops on

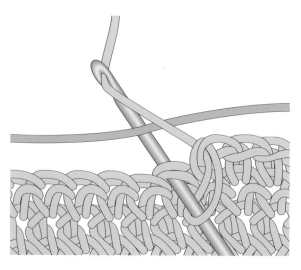

hook. Repeat from * 3 more times. Work the next stitch with the old yarn until 2 loops remain on the hook—regardless of the stitch you're working. Yarn over hook with the new yarn, and pull the new yarn through both loops. Continue across the row, crocheting with the new yarn over the tail of the old yarn. The ends will be woven in. Trim the ends close to the work. The illustration below shows the new yarn (dark green) from the wrong side of the work.

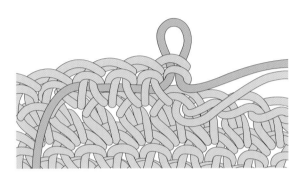

FASTENING OFF

When you have come to the end of the piece you're working, you'll need to cut the yarn.

TO WORK:
Enlarge the last loop of yarn with the hook to about 6", remove the hook, insert the scissors, cut the yarn from the ball, and tighten the tail gently. Weave in the ends and trim close to the work.

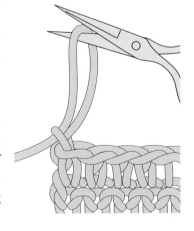

An alternative way to end the yarn is to cut the tail about 6" long and pull it through the last stitch. I don't recommend this because it leaves a knot at the corner of your work and you are actually making an extra chain stitch that can make finishing difficult.

UNDERSTANDING CROCHET INSTRUCTIONS

There are 2 types of crochet instruction formats—written and charted. We will cover both in this section.

When you first look at most patterns, you'll see that the following pertinent information is given at the top of the pattern.

+ Finished sizes

+ Type of yarn and how much to buy

+ Size of the hooks you'll need

+ Any accessories, such as buttons or zippers, that you'll need to finish your project

+ Stitch gauge and row gauge

Your first step after deciding what yarn to use will be to make a swatch for your stitch gauge (see page 37). With that completed, you can choose the pattern size to make and begin. Make the pieces in the order given in the directions.

Written Instructions

Crochet instructions are written in a sort of shorthand that uses abbreviations as well as parentheses, stars, or asterisks. This is done to make the pattern writing short and simple. All of this looks like a foreign language until you get used to it. You must work slowly and methodically until the directions become second nature. You may find it necessary to write them out word for word until you have all of the abbreviations memorized and fully understand all of the repeats.

ABBREVIATIONS:

Below are some of the abbreviations that you might see in crochet instructions.

approx	approximately	**pm**	place marker
beg	begin(ning)	**rem**	remaining
bl	back loop	**rep(s)**	repeat(s)
BP	back post	**rnd(s)**	round(s)
BPdc	back-post double crochet	**RS**	right side
		rsc	reverse single crochet
ch	chain or chain stitch	**sc**	single crochet
cont	continue(ing)	**sc2tog**	single crochet 2 together
dc	double crochet		
dc2tog	double crochet 2 together	**sk**	skip
		sl st	slip stitch
dec	decrease(ing)	**slst2tog**	slip stitch 2 together
fl	front loop		
FP	front post	**sp(s)**	space(s)
FPdc	front-post double crochet	**st(s)**	stitch(es)
		tch	turning chain
hdc	half double crochet	**tr**	treble crochet
hdc2tog	half double crochet 2 together	**tr2tog**	treble crochet 2 together
		tog	together
inc	increase(ing)	**WS**	wrong side
lp(s)	loop(s)	**YO**	yarn over hook
patt	pattern		

PARENTHESES:

Parentheses are used to group related information—such as measurements—or to group several steps that are to be repeated, or to sum up a group of steps that are to be worked in 1 stitch, as in the following examples:

S (M, L, XL)
(5 dc in next st, ch 2) 4 times
(sc, ch 1) 3 times

ASTERISKS OR STARS:

Asterisks may be located at the beginning of a direction or at the beginning and end of a direction that is to be repeated across the row or a certain number of times. You might see examples of both treatments in the same pattern.

Ch 2, hdc in next st, *dc in next st, hdc in next st, rep from * to end.
OR
Ch 2, hdc in next st, *dc in next st, hdc in next st, rep from * 5 times.
OR
Ch 2, hdc in next st, *dc in next st, hdc in next st*, rep from * to * 5 times.

Without the asterisks, the above directions would be written like this: Ch 2, hdc in next st, dc in next st, hdc in next st, dc in next st, hdc in next st; cont to work the dc in next st and hdc in next st until you reach the end of the row or complete the patt the required number of times. As you can see, the written directions are much longer and harder to follow.

Chart Instructions

Charts are the most simplified version of crochet instructions. They take some getting used to, but honestly they are very easy to follow once you understand them. Below are a few of the symbols you'll see for the basic stitches.

SYMBOL KEY

◯   Chain stitch (ch) (see page 13)

⬭   Slip stitch (sl st) (see page 16)

+   Single crochet (sc) (see page 17)

T   Half double crochet (hdc) (see page 19)

Ŧ   Double crochet (dc) (see page 20)

Ŧ   Treble crochet (tr) (see page 22)

⋏   Decrease 1 single crochet (sc2tog) (see page 41)

⋀   Decrease 1 half double crochet (hdc2tog) (see page 42)

⋀   Decrease 1 double crochet (dc2tog) (see page 42)

⋀   Decrease 1 treble crochet (tr2tog) (see page 43)

⋁   Increase 1 single crochet (see page 46)

⋁   Increase 1 half double crochet (see page 46)

⋁   Increase 1 double crochet (see page 46)

⋁   Increase 1 treble crochet (see page 46)

When following charted instructions, start at the bottom. Right-side rows (odd rows) are read from right to left and the row number is on the right. Wrong-side rows (even rows) are read from left to right, and the row number is on the left.

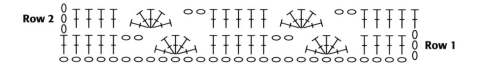

The written directions for the chart on the facing page are as follows:

Chain 31.

Row 1: Dc in 4th ch from hook, dc in each of next 3 ch, *sk 2 ch, work 5 dc in next ch (shell made), ch 2, sk 4 ch, work 1 dc in each of next 5 ch*, rep from * to * across, turn.

Row 2: Ch 3, work 1 dc in each of next 4 dc, *sk ch-2 sp, work 5 dc in first dc of shell, ch 2, sk 4 dc of shell, work 1 dc in each of next 5 dc, rep from * to * across. Rep row 2.

Compare the written directions to the chart as you work the sample. I think you'll find it easier to follow the chart since there are 5 double crochets that are worked separately and then 5 double crochets that are worked all in 1 stitch. It's easy to get confused. Of course, it's really great when patterns give you both the written and the charted version of the directions so that you can look at both if you're having trouble with one or the other.

Once you get a feel for charts, you may feel confident enough to create your own. Use graph paper and a pencil to draw each symbol in the correct row so that you know exactly where each stitch is supposed to be in relation to the stitch in the row below it. Start at the bottom with row 1 and work your way up.

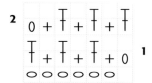

This is an example of drawing your own chart on ¼"-square graph paper.

Gauge

Gauge is by far the most important factor in getting crochet garments to fit or to make any crochet project come out the right size. The correct gauge is also essential to ensure that you have enough yarn for your project.

Let's do just a little math to make this clear. If your pattern tells you to get 5 single crochets to the inch and your pattern has 100 single crochets for the back, 100 divided by 5 equals 20. That means the back is supposed to measure 20" across. But if you're getting 4½ stitches to the inch, which doesn't sound like it's too far off, look at what happens to the width of the back: 100 single crochets divided by 4½ equals 22¼". This makes your back 2¼" too large. If the same thing happens on the front, then your whole sweater is 4½" too large. All that work and it doesn't fit—what a shame!

Here are the rules for getting the correct gauge.

+ Make a swatch at least 4" to 6" square so that you have lots of area to measure in.

+ Before you measure the swatch, wash or block the swatch in the same manner you intend to treat the garment after it has been worn.

+ The hook size in a pattern is just a recommendation; you may have to move up or down in hook size before your tension results in the correct gauge.

+ Stitch gauge has to be absolutely "right on." Row gauge can be slightly off since most lengths are measured.

+ Don't pull or tug on the swatch to get the gauge you need.

+ Measure the swatch flat and on a hard surface.

✦ Always measure in the middle of the swatch; the edges tend to be looser than the middle.

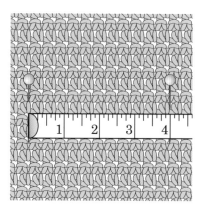

Measuring stitches

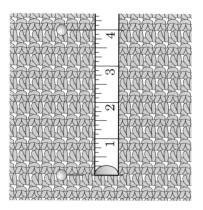

Measuring rows

✦ Redo the swatch, if necessary, until you achieve the correct gauge.

✦ As you work on a project, check the gauge frequently. Your bad day at work may show up in your crochet.

✦ Don't rip out your swatch to use in your project; save it to try out borders or buttonholes.

✦ Buy an extra skein of yarn, if necessary, to make sure you have enough, especially if you normally have to do a lot of swatching for the gauge.

Decreases

Simply stated, decreases take away stitches. You'll find them necessary for shaping armholes and necks in garments. In some pattern stitches, you'll make decreases in a row or a section and then make increases in another row or section to make up for the earlier stitch loss. These corresponding decreases and increases create some beautiful patterns across the width of the work.

INTERNAL DECREASES

In general, decreases are made by beginning the first stitch but not completing it, then beginning to make the next stitch and leaving all of the extra loops on the hook. You repeat this process for as many stitches as you want to decrease, and then with one final yarn over the hook you pull a loop through all of the loops on the hook to create one final stitch.

+ Internal decreases can be worked anywhere within the crochet fabric or at either end.

+ A smooth edge remains.

+ They will blend in with the stitches and be invisible.

+ They can be worked on the right side or wrong side.

+ One stitch remains after the final step is worked.

+ They are reversible.

Single crochet decreases

Half double crochet decreases

Double crochet decreases

Treble crochet decreases

All decreases are shown in white.

TO WORK SINGLE CROCHET DECREASE (sc2tog):

(Insert the hook into the next stitch, yarn over hook, and pull through stitch) twice (3 loops on hook), yarn over hook, and pull through all 3 loops on the hook.

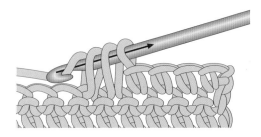

TO WORK HALF DOUBLE CROCHET DECREASE (hdc2tog):

(Yarn over hook, insert the hook into the next stitch, yarn over hook, and pull through stitch) twice (5 loops on hook), yarn over hook, and pull through all 5 loops on the hook.

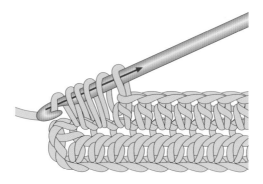

TO WORK DOUBLE CROCHET DECREASE (dc2tog):

Yarn over hook, insert the hook into the next stitch, yarn over hook and pull through stitch, yarn over hook and pull through 2 loops on the hook (2 loops on hook).

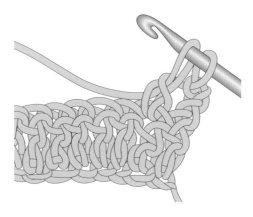

Yarn over hook, insert the hook into the next stitch, yarn over and pull through stitch, yarn over hook and pull through 2 loops on the hook (3 loops on hook).

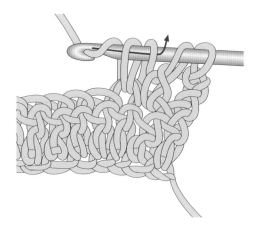

Yarn over hook and pull through all 3 loops on the hook.

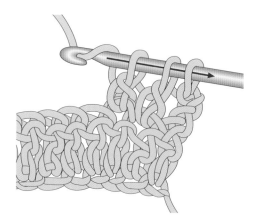

TO WORK TREBLE CROCHET DECREASE (tr2tog):
Yarn over hook twice, insert the hook into the stitch, yarn over hook, and pull through stitch (4 loops on hook). Yarn over hook and pull through 2 loops on the hook (3 loops on hook). Yarn over hook and pull through 2 loops on the hook (2 loops on hook). Yarn over hook twice, insert the hook into the next stitch, and pull through stitch (5 loops on hook). (Yarn over hook and pull through 2 loops on hook) twice (3 loops on hook). Yarn over hook and pull through the remaining 3 loops on the hook (1 loop on hook).

EXTERNAL DECREASES

External decreases are used in areas where you won't be using the stitches again. The best example is where you need a flat edge, such as a neck or an armhole opening.

Three stitches decreased at each end

+ External decreases create a very smooth edge.

+ They can be worked over any pattern stitch.

+ They are used for shaping.

+ There is no turning chain used.

+ Borders or neck bands can be added later if necessary.

+ They are reversible.

+ Once this decrease has been worked, the pattern stitch is no longer worked over it.

+ They can be worked on the right side or wrong side.

TO WORK AT THE BEGINNING OF A ROW:

Don't chain at the end of the previous row. Slip-stitch across the number of stitches you need to decrease plus 1. Chain for height and work across in pattern. The stitch you chained out of won't count as one of the decreased stitches.

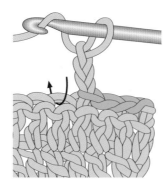

TO WORK AT THE END OF A ROW:

Work to the number of stitches you need to decrease, chain the appropriate number of stitches you need for height, turn, and continue in pattern.

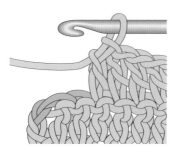

Increases

Increases are used for adding stitches. They can keep a circular or square piece flat when working in the round. In some pattern stitches, they are used to even out the row after decreases have been worked. Increases are also used for shaping an armhole or a sleeve.

INTERNAL INCREASES

Internal increases are worked by making the same stitch twice into 1 stitch from the previous row. You can work them one at a time for a subtle change to the shape of the row, or you can work several of them in 1 stitch to go around a corner. This is one time where you can insert your hook at the base of the turning chain to create a new stitch.

+ Internal increases create a smooth edge for borders.

+ They can be worked in any stitch pattern.

+ They can be worked on the right side or wrong side.

+ They are worked the same at the beginning or end of the row.

+ Done individually, they are very subtle within a row.

+ They are reversible.

Single crochet increase

Half double crochet increase

Double crochet increase

Treble crochet increase

All increases are shown in white.

TO WORK INCREASES:

Work to the designated stitch and work the required number of increases in that stitch. The increase is worked the same for all stitches. The illustration below shows a single crochet increase.

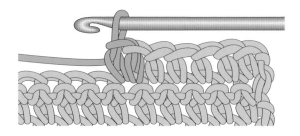

EXTERNAL INCREASES

External increases allow you to add many stitches at the beginning or end of the row. These would be used, for example, to make a T-shaped garment.

External increases at both ends

+ External increases create a smooth 45° angle at the edge of the crochet.

+ They can be worked in any stitch pattern.

+ They can be worked on the right side or wrong side.

+ They are used for shaping.

+ They are reversible.

TO WORK AT THE BEGINNING OF A ROW:

At the end of the last row before the increases are to be made, chain the number of stitches required for the increase, plus the number of chains required for the turning chain. Remember that the turning chain will count as a stitch for all stitches except single crochet. Work the pattern stitch across the new and old stitches.

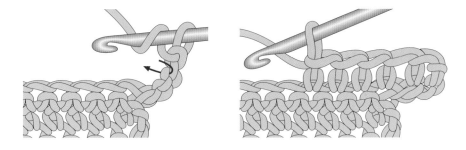

TO WORK AT THE END OF A ROW:

*Insert the hook into the base of the last stitch made.

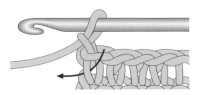

Yarn over hook and pull through stitch. Complete the stitch as usual. Repeat from * until the required number of stitches have been added. Chain for height, then turn, and proceed in the pattern stitch.

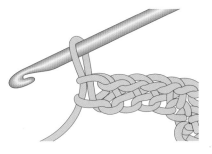

Seams

Believe it or not, seams and finishing can make or break any crochet that you do. This is the place where your project will shine when it's finished. Perfect seams and finishing are what change a project from something you wouldn't be caught dead in to something you can't wait to wear or display. I know that finishing isn't the favorite part for most crocheters, but if you follow the guidelines below, I guarantee you'll be much happier with the result.

All of the seam options are described here. You can use a combination of seaming methods on your garment or the same one on the entire garment. The woven seam is the best option for garments, while the other options are used mostly for afghans or children's clothing, where strength with a little bulk is an absolute must. I use the woven seam for all my garments except in special circumstances, such as when a shoulder seam—depending on the stitch used—lies better when I use a whipstitch or a slip-stitch seam.

Use your swatch to help you decide what seam is best for your garment. A little practice on some swatches is worth the time. You don't want to risk ruining the edges of your garment by stitching into them and then ripping out the stitches, leaving the edges slightly larger than they were to begin with. That would make the next seam you try even uglier. If you do have to rip out a seam, mist the edge with water and then let it dry before you try again. This will pull the stitches back to their original shape in most cases.

In general, always work the seams in the same yarn used for the crochet. There may be times, however, when the yarn is too bulky or has lumps and bumps that might make seaming difficult. In these cases, use a lighter-weight yarn in the same color and fiber content to decrease the bulk at the seams. And of course, choose a seam that produces as little bulk as possible.

Always use a blunt tapestry needle to sew the seams. If you use a sharp tapestry needle, you can split the yarn and decrease the amount of stretch in the seam. Use the sharp needle to weave in the ends instead; this is where you may want to split the yarn so that the ends won't come out!

Finishing takes time and patience. I recommend working at a table to help keep the edges flat and the seams from puckering. Use lots of coilless safety pins. It's better to overpin than not to pin a seam at all or to pin just a little bit. Below is a list of what you'll need before you start the job of assembling a garment.

+ Scissors

+ Blunt and sharp tapestry needles

+ A ball of yarn

+ Coilless safety pins

+ Crochet hook you used for project, and possibly other sizes if called for in your pattern

+ Tape measure or ruler

+ Pattern directions

+ Buttons or zipper, if applicable

+ All pieces blocked if required

STARTING YARN FOR SEAMING

There are several methods for starting yarn prior to seaming. The first 2 methods below are for slip-stitch and single crochet seaming. The start would be the same on a vertical edge. The methods on page 53 are for woven and whipstitch seaming.

WITH HOOK AND WITHOUT SLIPKNOT:

Holding both pieces with right sides together, insert the hook into the first stitch of each piece, pull a loop through, yarn over hook, and pull through loop on the hook, creating 1 chain stitch. Leave a 5" tail on the wrong side of the work.

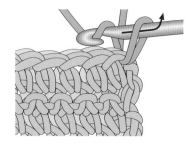

WITH HOOK AND WITH SLIPKNOT:

Make a slipknot on the hook, holding both pieces with right sides together, insert the hook into the first stitch of each piece, pull a loop through, yarn over hook, and pull through both loops. Leave tail about 5" long on the wrong side of the work.

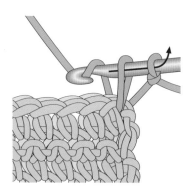

WITH NEEDLE AND NEW PIECE OF YARN:

Place right side of crochet pieces face up. Thread the yarn onto a tapestry needle. Insert the needle from back to front in the edge of the chain on the right-hand piece, leaving a 6" tail, and then *insert the needle from back to front into the edge of the chain of the piece on the left. Make a figure eight with the yarn and come back under the edge of the cast on for the piece on the right. Begin the seam.

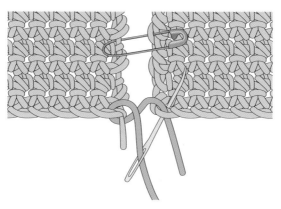

WITH NEEDLE AND YARN FROM STARTING CHAIN:

Place right side of crochet pieces face up. Thread the tail from the starting chain at the edge of the right-hand piece onto a tapestry needle, and continue from * above.

WOVEN SEAMS

Woven seams are worked with a yarn needle and yarn. These seams are virtually invisible and nonbulky.

Horizontal woven seam. Half of seam is pulled tight to show how completed seam will look.

Vertical woven seam. Half of seam is pulled tight to show how completed seam will look.

+ Woven seams can be worked on vertical and horizontal seams.

+ They're worked from the right side of the work, which allows you to see what is happening.

+ They work with all stitches.

+ They work well with all weights of yarn.

+ If the number of rows in each piece doesn't match, it's easy to "cheat" or adjust the alignment, if necessary, to make the rows line up.

TO WORK HORIZONTAL SEAMS (STITCHES TO STITCHES):

With right sides facing up, pin the edges together with coilless safety pins, keeping the edges flat and matching stitches from one piece to the other. Thread a blunt needle with about 20" of yarn or use the tail if long enough. Secure the yarn at the beginning of a piece, leaving about a 6" tail (see page 53).

+ On the top piece, insert the needle into the first chain at the beginning of the row and out the next chain, and pull through.

+ On the bottom piece, *insert the needle into the corresponding chain on the opposite piece and out the next chain, and pull through.*

+ Repeat from * to * until seam is completed. Pull the yarn gently to tighten the seam and bring the edges together. Fasten off. Weave in the ends and trim close to the work.

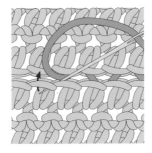

TO WORK VERTICAL SEAMS (ROWS TO ROWS):

With right sides facing up, pin the edges together with coilless safety pins, keeping the edges flat and matching rows from one piece to the other. Thread a blunt needle with about 20" of yarn or use the tail if long enough. Secure the yarn at the beginning of a piece, leaving about a 6" tail (see page 53).

✦ On the right piece, insert the needle from front to back and up to the front again under the first knot or post of the row, and pull through.

✦ On the left piece, insert the needle from front to back and up to the front again under the first knot or post of the row, and pull through.

✦ *On the right piece, insert the needle in the spot where you came out the previous time, go under a knot or post and up to the front again, and pull through.

✦ On the left piece, insert the needle in the spot where you came out the previous time on this side, go under a knot or post and up to the front again, and pull through.*

Repeat from * to *, working into corresponding rows on each side and making sure they match until the seam is completed. Pull the yarn gently to tighten the seam and bring the edges together. Fasten off. Weave in the ends and trim close to the work.

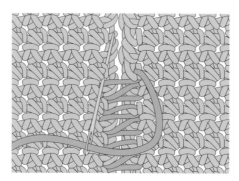

SLIP-STITCH SEAMS

Slip-stitch seams are worked with a crochet hook and yarn. They add little bulk to the seam.

Front of horizontal slip-stitch seam

Back of horizontal slip-stitch seam

Front of vertical slip-stitch seam

✦ Slip-stitch seams can be worked on vertical and horizontal seams.

✦ They leave a small gap on the right side between pieces.

✦ They must be done loosely to allow the seam to stretch.

✦ They're generally worked on the wrong side.

✦ They work well on sloped shoulders because they can be worked in a straight line, leaving a smooth seam.

✦ A slip-stitch seam can be worked as a decorative seam on the outside of the work.

✦ A slip-stitch seam can be used to join motifs, such as Granny Squares.

TO WORK HORIZONTAL SEAMS (STITCHES TO STITCHES):
With right sides together, pin the edges with coilless safety pins, matching stitches from one piece to the other. Use the same crochet hook as used for the project or, if you wish, use a hook one size larger to keep the seam loose. With a slipknot on the hook, *insert the hook under both loops, or the back loop only, of the stitch on the front piece and then into the corresponding loops on the back piece, yarn over hook, and pull through all the loops on the hook.* Repeat from * to * until the seam is complete, making sure to keep the stitches loose so that the seam has elasticity. Fasten off. Weave in the ends and trim them close to the work.

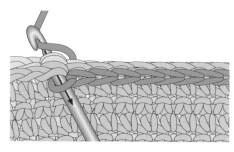

Illustration shows working into
both loops of each piece.

TO WORK VERTICAL SEAMS (ROWS TO ROWS):

Work as for horizontal seams, but work under the stitches at the ends of each row.

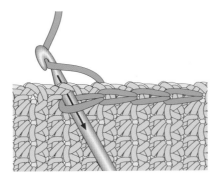

TO JOIN MOTIFS:

Work as for horizontal seams, working into the back loops only. The following photo shows 2 motifs joined by working into the back loops only.

SINGLE CROCHET SEAMS

Single crochet seams are very strong, but they add more bulk than any other seam.

Front of horizontal single crochet seam

Back of horizontal single crochet seam

Front of vertical single crochet seam

+ Single crochet seams can be worked on vertical and horizontal seams.

+ They're generally worked on the wrong side.

+ If worked from the right side, it will leave a decorative chain stitch.

+ They must be done loosely to allow for more elasticity and stretch.

TO WORK HORIZONTAL SEAM (STITCHES TO STITCHES):

With right sides together, pin the edges with coilless safety pins, matching stitches from one piece to the other. Use the same crochet hook as used for the project or, if you wish, use a hook one size larger to keep the stitches loose. With a slipknot on the hook, *insert the hook under 1 or both loops of the stitch on the front piece and then into the corresponding loop(s) on the back piece, yarn over hook, and work a single crochet stitch.* Repeat from * to * until the seam is completed, making sure to keep the stitches loose so that the seam has elasticity. Fasten off. Weave in the ends and trim close to the work.

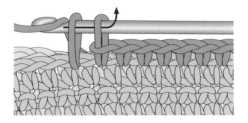

Illustration shows working under
both loops on each piece.

TO WORK VERTICAL SEAMS (ROWS TO ROWS):

Work as for horizontal seams, but work under the stitches at the ends of each row. Work more than 1 single crochet stitch per row if rows are half double crochet or double crochet.

WHIPSTITCH SEAMS

Whipstitch seams are worked with a yarn needle and yarn. They add very little bulk.

Front of horizontal whipstitch seam

Back of horizontal whipstitch seam

Front of vertical whipstitch seam

- ✦ Whipstitch seams can be worked on vertical and horizontal seams.

- ✦ They're worked on the wrong side and they show on the right side of the work.

- ✦ They look the same on the right and wrong side when completed.

- ✦ Tension must be even.

- ✦ They're good for attaching borders.

- ✦ They work well with thick or bulky yarns.

- ✦ They're good for straight seams.

- ✦ They can be used to join motifs such as Granny Squares.

TO WORK HORIZONTAL SEAMS
(STITCHES TO STITCHES):

With right sides together, pin the edges with coilless safety pins, matching stitches from one piece to the other. Thread a needle with about 20" of yarn or use the tail if it's long enough. Begin at the right edge and *insert the needle under the back loop of the back piece and the front loop of the front piece.* (Alternative: use both loops of both pieces.) Repeat from * to * until all stitches are whipstitched together across the edge. Fasten off. Weave in the ends and trim close to the work.

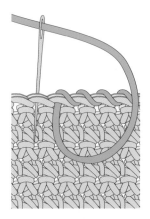

Illustration shows working under
both loops of each piece.

TO WORK VERTICAL SEAMS (ROWS TO ROWS):
Work as for horizontal seams, but work under the stitches at the ends of each row. Work more than 1 whipstitch per row if rows are half double or double crochet.

TO JOIN MOTIFS:
Follow the directions for working the horizontal seam on page 63. You can work with right sides together, or with right sides facing up as shown in the illustration.

The following photo shows 2 motifs joined by working into the back loops only.

ASSEMBLING A SWEATER

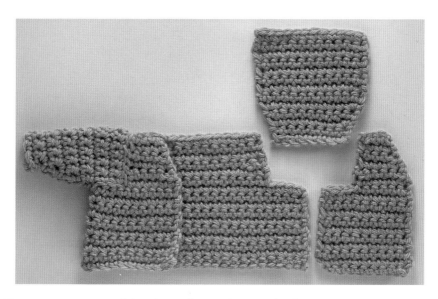

You can use a combination of seaming methods on your sweater. For example, if your shoulder has stair steps, you may want to slip-stitch them together for a smoother seam. And the side seams might look better with a woven seam. The object is to make the seams as invisible as possible, using the best seaming methods to do this.

Below is the usual order in which pieces are put together. Some patterns will tell you to block pieces before putting the garment together. If you do, be sure all matching seams stay the same length. Measure each piece.

1. Sew shoulder seams.

2. Sew sleeves into armholes (skip for a vest).

3. Sew side seams from bottom edge to armhole.

4. Sew sleeve seams from cuff to armhole (skip for a vest).

5. Work front band, neck band, and buttonhole bands, or armhole bands if a vest.

6. Weave in the ends and trim close to the work.

7. Sew on pockets or any embellishments, such as buttons or zippers.

Using the woven-seam method, I've included an example of how you'd sew a simple sweater together. After blocking all of the pieces, if needed, lay them out on a flat surface with all of the supplies at hand.

TO SEW SHOULDER SEAM:
Pin in place. Weave the seam from the shoulder to the neck, using a tail or cutting a new piece of yarn. You can weave in the ends now, or wait until later.

 If you always start with the same shoulder when you put a sweater together, then the same sleeve and side seam, you'll have no difficulty finding the ends and knowing where to start ripping from if you end up taking the sweater apart for some reason.

TO SEW SLEEVE INTO ARMHOLE:
Fold the sleeve in half and find the center top. Pin the center top of the sleeve to the shoulder seam, and then pin the sleeve along each side. Cut a piece of yarn about 36" long. Starting at the shoulder seam and using only half the length of yarn, weave the seam going down the edge of half of the sleeve. This will feel quite different at first because you'll be sewing stitches to rows, and then it will be rows to rows, just like a side seam. Fasten off. With the other half of the yarn, finish the other half of the sleeve seam. Fasten off.

TO SEW SIDE SEAM:
Pin the side seam, matching rows. Weave the side seam from the bottom edge to the underarm. Fasten off.

TO SEW SLEEVE SEAM:
Pin the sleeve seam, matching rows. Weave the sleeve seam from the cuff to the underarm. Fasten off.

TO FINISH:
Sew on any borders, pockets, or collars as directed in the pattern.

Bands

In most cases, once you've crocheted a garment piece you'll need to add a band around the edges to prevent them from curling and growing longer than the rest of the garment. Crocheted bands are particularly helpful in stabilizing the edges of lacy or loose pattern stitches. If you need to add buttonholes or button loops to a piece of crocheted fabric, you'll usually work them on a band.

Bands can be worked in basic stitches or in decorative pattern stitches. The rules are the same for both.

BASIC BANDS

+ When making the garment, be sure the matching edges have the same number of rows or stitches.

+ Don't block before adding the band or border; instead, block everything at once.

+ The band is often worked with a smaller hook than what was used for the body; be sure to do a sample first using your gauge swatch.

+ Divide the area where you're placing the band into quarters, and mark with a safety pin to make it easier to get the same amount of stitches in each section.

+ For necklines and armholes, you may need to decrease a few times to keep them flat.

+ It's best to start the band with a row of single crochet and then go to a decorative edge (see page 70). Be sure you have the correct amount of stitches for a decorative edge to fit.

+ If the band is to be worked in another color, work the first row in the color of the garment. Then work the remaining rows of the band in the second color.

TO WORK FRONT BAND ALONE:

With right side facing you, join new yarn and single crochet in every other row or in every 3 out of 4 rows. Turn and continue in single crochet, or work the fancy border pattern.

TO WORK BOTTOM BAND ALONE:

With right side facing you, join new yarn at the corner and single crochet in every stitch across the bottom. If working in every stitch results in a slightly flared edge, try working in 3 out of every 4 stitches. Turn and continue in single crochet, or work a fancy border pattern.

TO WORK NECK BAND ALONE:

With right side facing you, join new yarn at the right front corner of neck and single crochet in each stitch around the edge. Decrease, if necessary, to keep the neck edge flat. Turn and continue in single crochet, or work a fancy border pattern.

TO WORK FRONT, BOTTOM, AND NECK BAND ALL AT ONE TIME:

With right sides facing you and starting at the right side seam, single crochet across the bottom to the right front corner, work 3 single crochets in the corner (if the yarn is heavy, work 2 single crochets), single crochet up the front of the sweater (if there is a corner for the neck, work 3 single crochets in the corner), single crochet around the neck and repeat around for the other side of the sweater. When you reach your first stitch, join with a slip stitch. Here you have the option of turning or working in rounds, or working a chain for height and continuing with the right side facing you. Continue to place 3 stitches in the corners. Double-check the band as it gets wider to be sure it's lying flat.

*Band on front edge
and along V neck*

*Band on front edge and starting
around a round neck*

TO WORK ARMHOLE BAND:

With right side facing you and starting at the side seam, single crochet around the armhole, making sure each side has the same number of stitches. If you find the armhole is too large, decrease only on the back side of the armhole to make the armhole fit better. The armhole band can also be worked in the round if the side seams are sewn together.

Band around armhole edge

DECORATIVE EDGES

After you have worked a basic band around the project, you may find that you'd like to add something extra special on the last row for the ultimate finishing touch. Below are 4 options.

Crab Stitch (or Reverse Single Crochet)

This stitch creates a raised beadlike edge. It's worked from left to right; in other words, with the right side facing you and from the end of the row back to the beginning of the row.

Single-crochet crab stitch

TO WORK:

Refer to the figures below. Chain 1, do not turn the work, *insert the hook toward the right into the next stitch (fig. 1), yarn over hook and pull through stitch (fig. 2); yarn over hook and pull through 2 loops on the hook (fig. 3).* Do not change the order of the stitches on the hook; the second loop on the hook is in front of the first loop and will cause the final "bump" when the stitch is completed. Repeat from * to * across row. Fasten off.

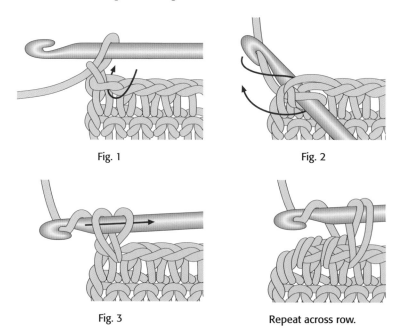

Fig. 1

Fig. 2

Fig. 3

Repeat across row.

Half-Double-Crochet Crab Stitch

This stitch is worked just like regular crab stitch but with a half double crochet instead. This will create a deeper and bulkier stitch on the border of the crochet.

Half-double-crochet crab stitch

Shell Stitch

The shell stitch adds a nice feminine touch to the edges of a garment. Be sure you have the correct number of stitches for the multiple. If not, you'll have to decrease or increase along the row before you start the shell stitch to make the border fit.

Shell-stitch border

TO WORK:
At the beginning of the next right-side row, single crochet in the first stitch, *skip 2 stitches, work 5 double crochets in the next stitch, skip 2 stitches, and single crochet in the next stitch.* Repeat from * to * to the end of the row. Fasten off.

Finding the Correct Number of Stitches for Pattern Multiple

Here's an example of how to use simple math to figure out how many stitches you'll need to work a particular pattern stitch that has a specific multiple.

If you want to add a shell-stitch border after the first band, you'll need to make sure that the multiple of 6 plus 1 will work out evenly into the number of stitches in your band. Any adjustments to the stitch count should be made on the row before you start the shell stitch. Count the number of stitches on the row that you'll be working for the band; let's say it's 52 stitches. Divide 52 by 6 and you get 8 plus 4 stitches left over ($52 \div 6 = 8.67$; $6 \times 8 = 48$; $52 - 48 = 4$). You only need 1 stitch left over to get to the multiple of 6 plus 1. So you'll need to decrease 3 stitches so that you have 49 stitches, which is divisible by 6 and gives us the perfect number—8 repeats with a remainder of 1 stitch.

Picots

This stitch creates small little bumps or picots along the edge of your work. They can be worked in every other stitch or with more stitches in between. When they're worked close together, they have a tendency to make the edge flare slightly. Be sure to use a smaller hook to prevent this or space the picots farther apart.

Picot border

TO WORK:

Picot: Work a single crochet, chain 3, and slip-stitch into the third chain from the hook.

After working a foundation of single crochet, on the next right-side row: (single crochet in the next 2 stitches, make a picot) to the last 2 stitches, and single crochet in the last 2 stitches.

Once again, you'd have to make the multiple fit the number of stitches you have. If you want to increase the number of stitches between the picots, change the number of stitches you single crochet into before and after you make the picot.

Buttonholes and Button Loops

Buttonholes and button loops can be used as a closure on many items, including garments, purses, and backpacks. They can also be used as a decorative feature on projects such as children's toys.

BUTTONHOLES

Buttons are the most common way to close the front of a garment. Buttonholes are simple to work in any size, and they can be either vertical or horizontal. Both methods yield a stretchy buttonhole, so be careful to make a sample first to be sure the buttonhole doesn't end up too large. The buttonhole can also be reinforced to secure its size and make it easy to find (see page 78). The decision to make one over the other has a lot to do with how much room you have.

Buttonholes should be worked in a firm stitch, such as single or half double crochet. The idea is to have a sturdy background stitch to support the buttonhole on one side and the button on the other side.

Vertical buttonhole

Horizontal buttonhole

Vertical Buttonholes

+ ✦ Vertical buttonholes are worked in 2 parts, requiring 2 balls of yarn.

+ ✦ They take less room than horizontal buttonholes.

+ ✦ They can be made any size.

+ ✦ They work well with any yarn.

+ ✦ They may require reinforcing.

+ ✦ They can be worked while the garment is being worked.

+ ✦ They can be made in a separate band and attached to the garment.

TO WORK:

Crochet to the row where the buttonhole is to be placed, ending with a completed right side row. Chain for height, work the number of stitches to where the buttonhole is to be placed, turn, and chain for height. Continue in the pattern on those stitches only, working an odd number of rows required for the height of the buttonhole. Don't fasten off, but leave a large loop on the left-hand edge of the first section of the buttonhole so that it won't pull out.

With right side facing you, attach the second ball of yarn, skipping 1 stitch from the first section of the buttonhole. Work 1 row less than the first section and fasten off. To close buttonhole, go back to the first side of the buttonhole and insert the hook in the loop, chain 1 at join, and continue across the second section.

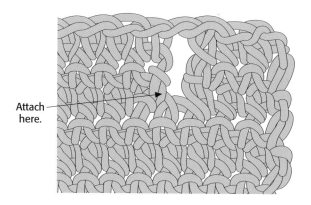

Attach here.

On the next row, work across the row in the pattern, working a stitch in the chain 1. Continue in the pattern as established.

 Tip: For a tighter buttonhole, don't skip a stitch before working the second section of the buttonhole, and then don't chain 1 at the join when closing the buttonhole.

If you're working this buttonhole as a vertical buttonhole in a band that will be attached to the garment, you can use a smaller crochet hook for the whole band to prevent the band and the buttonhole from stretching.

Horizontal Buttonholes

✦ Horizontal buttonholes take more room than vertical buttonholes.

✦ They can be made any size.

✦ They work well with any yarn.

✦ They may require reinforcing.

✦ They can be worked while the garment is being worked.

✦ When worked in a band crocheted on the front and neck edges, they will appear vertical.

TO WORK:

Crochet to area where buttonhole is to be placed. Work 1 chain for each stitch you're skipping for the desired length of the buttonhole (for example, if you skip 3 stitches in the previous row, then chain 3 stitches), and continue in pattern as established. On the return row, continue in pattern, working the same number of pattern stitches into the chain space as were skipped.

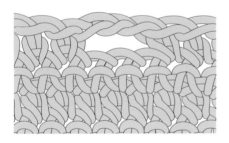 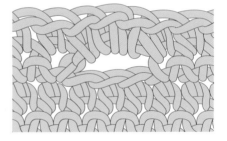

Reinforcing Buttonholes

The buttonhole stitch can be used to stabilize and strengthen any buttonhole. Reinforcing will reduce the size of the buttonhole slightly. It works with all yarns; however, if the yarn is very thick, separate the plies to decrease the bulk.

Buttonhole stitch

Reinforced buttonhole

TO WORK:

Using the same yarn you crocheted the item with, cut a piece about 20" long and thread it onto a blunt needle. Starting at the lower right end of the buttonhole, anchor the tail by going under a stitch on the wrong side of the work, but leave the tail long enough to be woven in later. *From the right side, insert the needle into the crochet and out the space of the buttonhole toward the left, making sure the needle comes out on top of the yarn loop*. Continue from * to * to the end of the buttonhole, turn, work the upper edge of the buttonhole, turn, and join to where you began. Be sure all the buttonholes are done evenly with the same amount of stitches.

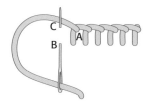

BUTTON LOOPS

Button loops are an alternative to buttonholes and are used to close garments, purses, and other crocheted items. There are 2 types: a 1-row button loop is worked on the last row of a band, and a 2-row button loop is worked on the last 2 rows of a band or at the top of a purse that is drawn closed with cording that runs through the loops.

1-row button loop

2-row button loop

+ Button loops create a looser closure than buttonholes made within the crochet because the front bands of the garment won't sit on top of each other.

+ They are not recommended for a button larger than 2".

+ They must be worked on the finishing edge of a garment as a band is being crocheted around the fronts and neck.

+ They are the perfect finish for a light, lacy garment, because they are airy looking, like the pattern stitch in the garment.

TO WORK 1-ROW BUTTON LOOP:

Before the final row of the band is completed, mark the beginning and ending stitch for each button loop with a safety pin. Single crochet to the second mark made for the first button loop.

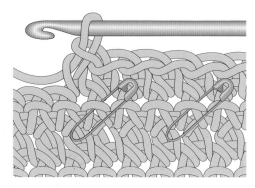

Right side of work

*Turn, chain the number of stitches required for the button to go through, and slip-stitch to the first marked stitch, which is the beginning of the button loop.

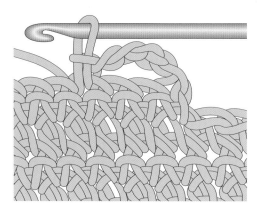

Wrong side of work

Turn, chain 1, and work the same number of single crochets into the chain space as the number of chains in the loop. For example, if you chained 5 stitches for the loop, single crochet 5 stitches in the chain space. Single crochet across the row or to the next marked place (second safety pin) for the next loop and repeat from *. Finish the row.

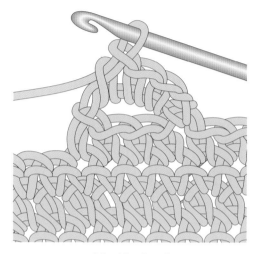

Right side of work

TO WORK 2-ROW BUTTON LOOP:

Crochet the band until there are only 2 more rows remaining. Mark the stitch where the button loop is to be placed. Single crochet to the mark for the first button loop, *chain the number of stitches required to accommodate the button, single crochet into the next stitch, single crochet across the row or to the next button loop, and repeat from *. On the next row, single crochet to the first button loop, **work the same number of single crochets into the chain space as the number of chains in the loop. For example, if you chained 5 stitches for the loop, single crochet 5 stitches in the chain space. Continue across the row or to the next loop and repeat from **. Finish the row.

CALCULATING
BUTTONHOLE PLACEMENT

Use the following chart to help you figure out how to place evenly spaced buttonholes in a garment. This formula will work for any type of buttonhole, including button loops, you want to use.

Number of stitches in buttonhole band	_____ A
Number of stitches used for each buttonhole (for button loops this will be zero)	_____ B
Total number of buttonholes	_____ C
Multiply B by C	_____ D
Subtract D from A	_____ E
Number of stitches before first, and after last, buttonhole	_____ F
Subtract F from E	_____ G

G = total number of stitches between all buttonholes

Subtract 1 from C to get number of spaces between buttonholes	_____ H
Divide G by H	_____ I

I = number of stitches between each buttonhole

You'll need to have a whole number at the end of the formula (I); a fraction won't work. If there is a remainder, place the extra stitches before the first or after the last buttonhole, or equally distribute them between the buttonholes.

Zippers

Zippers are another excellent closure for garments. They work perfectly in heavier sweaters, such as jackets and sturdy vests. They can also be used at the neck of a crewneck pullover.

*Zipper sewn to front of crochet followed by
1 row of single crochet and 1 row of crab stitch.*

Zippers aren't always available in the exact length of a garment opening, but it's easy to trim them to the right size.

TO TRIM A ZIPPER:

Measure the opening. Be careful that you don't stretch the crochet as you measure. Mark the zipper where you'd like it to end on the garment. At the top of the zipper, zigzag by sewing machine or overcast by hand about ¼" past where the zipper fits into the opening. Cut the zipper about 1" past the overcast area. Trim the teeth away on the excess part of the zipper, fold down, and sew the remaining tape to the wrong side of the zipper.

TO SEW A ZIPPER INTO A GARMENT:

When you have completed the final edge on the garment where the zipper will be placed, you're ready to insert the zipper. It's essential that the 2 edges are the same length and have the same number of stitches for the zipper to fit properly.

Using a fine crochet thread or yarn in a contrasting color, whipstitch the 2 edges together, matching stitch for stitch. Using sewing thread in a contrasting color, baste the zipper in place to the wrong side of the opening. Then with matching sewing thread and also on the wrong side, backstitch the zipper in place.

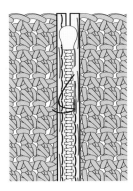

Remove the whipstitch from the front edge. Backstitch the zipper on the right side between the front crochet edge and the zipper teeth. Whip-stitch the loose edge of the zipper tape on the back to the garment. Tack down any areas that may get more stress or feel loose. Remove the remaining basting.

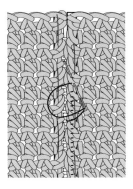

Pockets

I just love pockets! I have cold hands, and when I don't have gloves handy I think pockets are the next best thing. They are easily worked on a sweater while crocheting or placed as an afterthought when the sweater is finished. There are 2 types of pockets; patch pockets and slash pockets. They both can be made either vertical or horizontal.

PATCH POCKETS OR AFTERTHOUGHT POCKETS

Patch pockets are the easiest pockets to make.

Patch or afterthought pocket

TO WORK:

Make a square/rectangular piece of crochet, usually in the same stitch pattern as the sweater. Mark the placement on the sweater with the pocket located slightly closer to the side seam than the front. Sew the pocket with a whipstitch (see page 62) or woven seam (see page 54) to the front of the sweater and secure the top corners.

HORIZONTAL SLASH POCKETS

Horizontal slash pockets have to be planned. You must know exactly what row you want to place it on and exactly where on the row. It will be similar to making a large horizontal buttonhole.

Horizontal slash pocket. So that you can see the pocket lining, the sample does not show a band on the edge of the opening .

TO WORK:

Work in pattern to where the pocket is to be placed. Chain the number of stitches required to make the pocket opening, skip the same number of stitches across the previous row, and continue across the row in pattern. On the next row, work a stitch in each chain from the previous row so that the number of stitches for the front stays the same. Finish the piece.

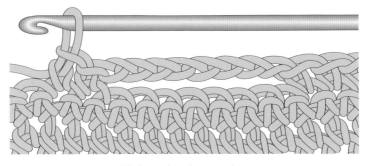

Horizontal pocket opening

POCKET LINING:

Working on the wrong side with the front upside down, single crochet across the stitches that were chained and continue until the pocket lining is long enough. This can be worked in finer yarn to decrease bulk. When the pocket lining is long enough, fasten off. Whipstitch the lining to the underside of the body.

Pocket lining on horizontal pocket (wrong side)

OPTIONAL BAND:

A band can be added to the front edge of the pocket opening if desired by crocheting across the stitches that were skipped for about 1". Tack down corners of band securely.

VERTICAL SLASH POCKET

This pocket also requires preplanning. You must know at which row you want to start and end the pocket, as well as the stitch where you want to separate the front into 2 pieces. You will work each side separately until the pocket opening is as long as you want it to be, and then rejoin the 2 sides and work the front as 1 piece again. It will be similar to working a large vertical buttonhole.

Vertical slash pocket from the right side. So that you can see the pocket lining, the sample does not show a band on the edge of the opening.

TO WORK:

Work in pattern to where the pocket is to be placed. Turn, and working only on the one side, continue until the pocket length is obtained, ending with completed right side row. Do not cut yarn, but leave a large loop on the left edge so that it won't pull out. You can also cut the yarn if desired and reattach it later.

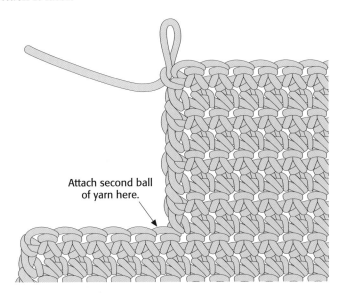

Attach second ball of yarn here.

With the right side facing you, attach the second ball of yarn in the next stitch to the left of the first side of the pocket opening. Work 1 row less than the first side and fasten off. To close the pocket, pick up the loop with the right side facing you and continue across the second section.

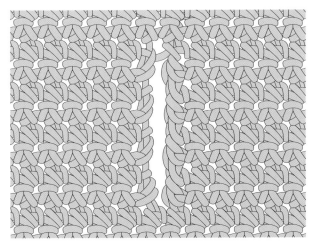

Two sides of pocket joined

Remember to work any shaping for the garment that might be necessary while you are working the pockets.

POCKET LINING:

Working sideways and on the wrong side, single crochet across the rows of the opening closest to the side seam and continue until the pocket lining is wide enough. This can be worked in finer yarn to decrease bulk. When the pocket lining is wide enough, fasten off. Whipstitch the lining to the underside of the front.

Pocket lining on vertical pocket (wrong side)

OPTIONAL BAND:

A band can be added to the edge of the pocket on the right side if desired by crocheting across the rows of the top piece for about 1". Tack down the corners of the band securely.

NOTE: *The vertical slash pocket can also be worked on a side seam. Leave the side seam open where you want the pocket, and crochet the pocket lining from the edge of the back piece toward the front piece.*

Working in the Round

Many crochet items begin in the center with a ring or circle of crochet. There are 2 methods for starting crochet in the center to work a project in the round. The first method begins with a chain of stitches that are joined to form a ring, and then stitches are worked into this ring. The second method begins with a short chain of stitches, and all the stitches for the first round are worked into the last chain. Both methods work equally well.

WORKING INTO A CHAIN RING

Working into a chain ring leaves a slightly larger hole than working into a chain stitch.

Single crochet worked in chain ring

TO WORK:

Chain 4 to 6 stitches, depending on how many stitches you're going to place in the ring after it's joined. Join with a slip stitch to the first chain made.

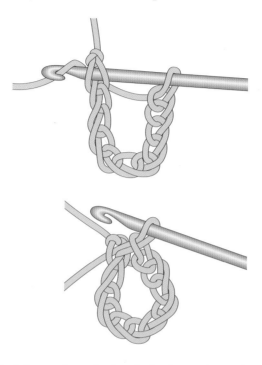

Chain for height, and work the desired number of stitches into the ring. Join with a slip stitch at the end of the row. The illustration is worked in double crochet.

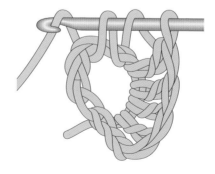

WORKING INTO A CHAIN STITCH

Working into a chain stitch leaves a smaller hole than working into a chain ring. It's probably the most common method because of the smaller hole.

Single crochet worked in a chain stitch

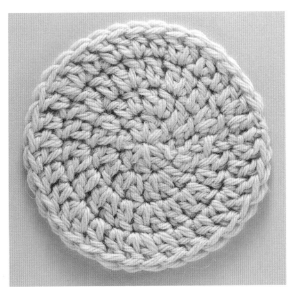

Double crochet worked in a chain stitch

TO WORK:

Chain the number of stitches required for the height of the stitch you're going to place in the hole, plus 1 more to place the rest of the stitches in. For example, with double crochet, you'd chain 2 or 3 for height, plus 1, for a total of 3 or 4.

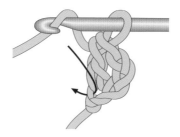

Work the desired number of double crochets into the third or fourth chain from hook, moving around the stitch.

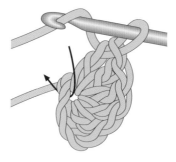

Join with a slip stitch to the top of the "chain 2 or 3" when completed.

INCREASING IN THE ROUND

Once you've made the center of the circle, you'll need to work increases at regular intervals to make the circle larger and to keep it flat. There may be a stitch pattern incorporated into the increases, for instance, when making a lace doily or even a Granny Square, but the increases still have to occur or the item won't lie flat. Refer to "Increases" on page 46 for information on how to work increases for the basic stitches. The following chart will guide you through the first few rounds of your circle.

Round	How to Work Increases
1 and 2	Increase 1 stitch in each stitch around.
3	Increase 1 stitch in every second stitch around.
4	Increase 1 stitch in every third stitch around.
5	Increase 1 stitch in every fourth stitch around.

Continue to increase in this manner, and your round crochet item will always lie flat. The pattern directions for round crochet items will always calculate this for you. If you're working on your own design, use the above chart to get started.

JOINING ROUNDS

There are 3 methods for joining rounds when working a circle, depending on whether you're working in a concentric circle or in a spiral.

**TO JOIN ROUNDS FOR A
CONCENTRIC CIRCLE WITHOUT TURNING:**

In this method, you'll *join the last stitch of every round to the first stitch of the previous round with a slip stitch. Chain for height and continue around, increasing as needed, until you get to the end of the next round*, and repeat from * to *. Working this way creates a visible seam where you join rounds and chain for height. On the last round, slip-stitch into the first stitch of the previous round and fasten off.

Rounds worked in a concentric circle without turning

**TO JOIN ROUNDS FOR A CONCENTRIC CIRCLE
WITH TURNING AT END OF EVERY ROW:**

In this method, you'll join the last stitch of every round to the first stitch of the previous round with a slip stitch and then turn the work after the slip-stitch join and before chaining for height. The result of this method is that you'll end up with a truly reversible piece of crochet without any right or wrong side.

Rounds worked in concentric circle with turning

TO JOIN ROUNDS FOR A SPIRAL:

In this method, you don't join the end of one round to another. You simply crochet around and around, increasing as needed in each round. To keep track of the rounds, use a stitch marker to mark the last stitch of a round. When you get to the last stitch, remove the marker, work the stitch, and replace the marker into the new last stitch before continuing the next round. After you've completed all the rounds for the circle, join the last stitch of the last round to the first stitch of the previous round with a slip stitch and fasten off.

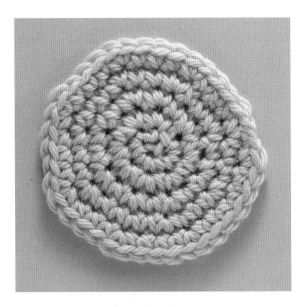

Rounds worked in a spiral

Filet Crochet

I love filet crochet! Worked as a group of "blocks" of double crochet and "empty blocks," known as spaces, filet crochet is normally used to depict pictures or letters. While it's most commonly worked in size 10 cotton crochet thread, it works just as well in heavier yarns for sweaters, afghans, or borders. Below are 2 samples of filet crochet in the same pattern to show you the vast difference between using crochet thread and worsted-weight yarn.

This sample is made in size 10 cotton crochet thread with a size 5 steel hook.

This sample is made in worsted-weight yarn with a size H hook.

The directions for filet crochet are usually given in chart form (see "Chart Instructions" on page 35), and once you understand the very few rules involved with the pattern stitch, you'll find the chart is the easiest way to work the pattern. Any picture or drawing that can be depicted in a graph format can be made in filet crochet. The chart can be made two ways, either in symbols or as empty squares (spaces) and filled-in squares (blocks). The second method is most common in pattern books. In this method, a space is equal to 2 chains and 1 double crochet, and a square is equal to 3 double crochets. I use ¼" graph paper to chart my designs. Here is an example of the sample on the facing page charted in both methods.

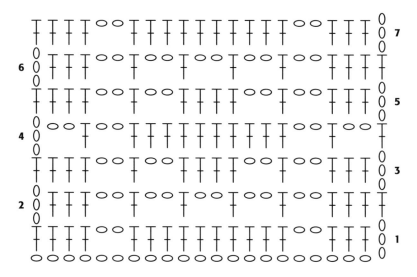

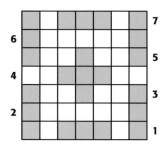

Filled-in squares are blocks
and empty squares are spaces.

HOW MANY STITCHES DO I CHAIN?

The number of chains to make at the beginning of a pattern depends on how many squares (blocks and spaces) are in the pattern and whether the first square after the chain is a block or a space.

IF THE FIRST SQUARE IS A BLOCK:

Multiply the number of squares by 3, and then add 3 stitches for the turning chain. For example, if you want 5 squares, 5 x 3 = 15, plus 3 for the turning chain = 18 chains. So you'd chain 18, start with a double crochet in the fourth chain from the hook, and then double crochet in the next chain to complete the first block and continue across the row.

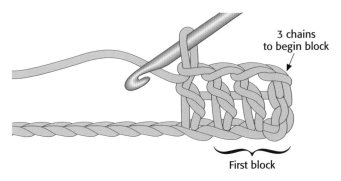

3 chains
to begin block

First block

IF THE FIRST SQUARE IS A SPACE:

Multiply the number of squares by 3, and then add 5 chains (3 for the turning chain and 2 for the top of the space). Using the same example from above, if you want 5 squares, 5 x 3 = 15, plus 5 for the turning chain and top of the space = 20 chains. So you'd chain 20 and work a double crochet in the eighth chain from the hook to complete the first space. To make the next space, skip 2 chains, chain 2, and double crochet in the next chain.

8 chains
to create
first space

First space

BLOCKS AND SPACES

Each block and space is made up of 3 stitches, and all turning chains are 3 chains.

Blocks and spaces in filet crochet

BLOCKS:

Three double crochets make 1 block. If the square below is a block, work a double crochet in each of the next 3 double crochets. If the square below is a space, work 2 double crochets in the space, and then work a double crochet in the next double crochet for a total of 3 double crochets.

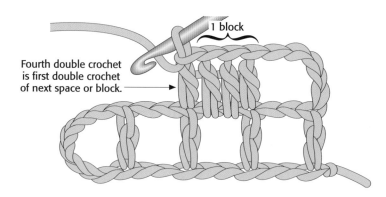

1 block

Fourth double crochet is first double crochet of next space or block. →

NOTE: *A block followed by a space will always have 4 double crochets because the fourth double crochet is the beginning double crochet for the next space. This is extremely important to remember and can prevent many errors.*

SPACES:

Two chains and 1 double crochet make 1 space. If the square below is a space, chain 2, skip the space below, and double crochet in the next double crochet. If the square below is a block, chain 2, skip the next 2 stitches, and double crochet in the next double crochet.

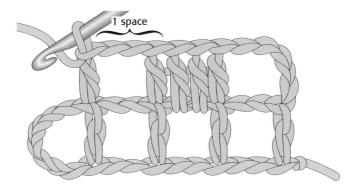

NOTE: *Always end the row with a double crochet, whether it ends with a space or a block. This is crucial in preventing errors, and all patterns assume this.*

DECREASES

Decreases are generally worked by decreasing an entire space or block instead of a single stitch, as in plain or patterned crochet.

Decrease at beginning of row

Decrease at end of row

TO DECREASE A SPACE OR BLOCK AT BEGINNING OF ROW:

Instead of making the required turning chain, slip-stitch across the required number of stitches for the number of blocks or spaces you want to decrease plus 1, make the turning chain, and continue across the row. You'll slip-stitch across 3 stitches for each space or block to be decreased.

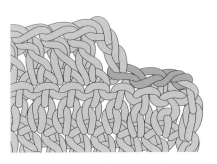

Decrease block at beginning of row.

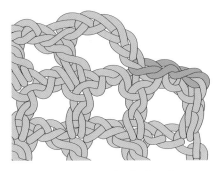

Decrease space at beginning of row.

TO DECREASE A SPACE OR BLOCK AT END OF ROW:

Work to the end of the row, leaving the number of blocks or spaces you want to decrease unworked, turn, make turning chain, and resume pattern. You must end with a complete block or space before turning.

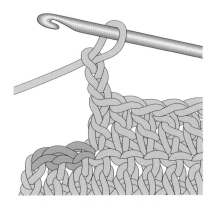

Decrease block at end of row.

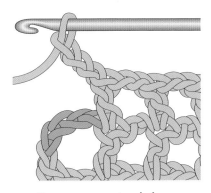

Decrease space at end of row.

INCREASES

The same idea for decreases applies to increases; a whole block or space is added to the beginning or end of the row.

Increase space at beginning and end of row

Increase block at beginning and end of row

TO INCREASE A SPACE AT BEGINNING OF ROW:

For 1 space, chain 8 (3 chains for the bottom, 3 chains for the turning chain, and 2 chains for the top of the space), and double crochet in the first double crochet. For 2 spaces or more, chain 3 for each space to be added, plus 5 chains (for the turning chain and top of space). For example, to increase 3 spaces, chain 9 (3 x 3), plus 5 chains = 14 chains. Double crochet in the eighth chain from the hook, and continue in pattern across row.

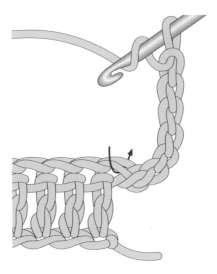

TO INCREASE A SPACE AT END OF ROW:

Chain 2, yarn over 3 times, insert hook into the base of the last double crochet, (yarn over hook and pull through 2 loops) 4 times (1 loop remains on hook). Repeat for each space to be added, working into the base of the last stitch.

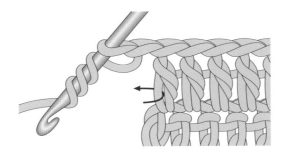

TO INCREASE A BLOCK AT BEGINNING OF ROW:

For the first block increase, chain 2, and for each additional block, chain 3, then chain 3 more for the turning chain. For example, if you're only increasing 1 block, chain 5 (2 + 3). To increase 3 blocks, chain 2 for the first block, chain 6 for the 2 additional blocks (2 x 3 = 6), and then chain 3 for the turning chain (2 + 6 + 3 = 11 chains). Double crochet in the fourth chain from the hook, double crochet in each of the next 2 chains to complete the first block, and then continue in the pattern across the row.

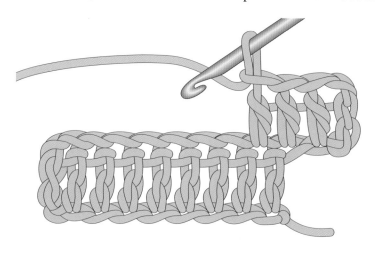

TO INCREASE A BLOCK AT END OF ROW:

For each block to be added, work a loose double crochet into the base of the last double crochet, and then work 2 double crochets into the base of each preceding double crochet.

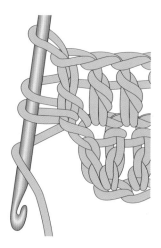

Intarsia

Intarsia is one of my favorite techniques and can be done in any of the basic crochet stitches. This technique will allow you to use many colors in your work without carrying strands of yarn across the back. You can add vertical stripes, simple squares, or even flowers to your work once you've mastered this technique.

Intarsia crochet

Patterns for intarsia are usually worked from a chart because the chart is easier to follow than directions written out line by line. At right is the chart I used for the sample worked in single crochet shown above.

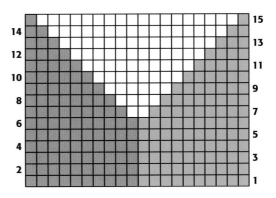

Read right-side rows or odd-numbered rows from right to left, and wrong-side rows or even-numbered rows from left to right.

NOTE: *Some charts use symbols to represent different colors. You'd have to match the symbol to the color on an index that would come with the pattern.*

TO WORK:

Wind each color onto a bobbin or into a butterfly (see facing page). These will hang from the back of your work while the colors are worked across the row. Work to the stitch before you're to change colors, leaving the last 2 loops of the stitch on the hook. Bring the new color up on the wrong side of the work. Yarn over hook with the new color and pull the new color through.

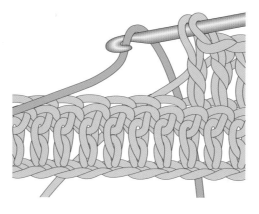

Drop the old color on the wrong side of the work. Pull the 2 tails tightly so that there is no gap or hole where the colors joined. When working on either side, be sure all the colors are brought up and dropped off on the wrong side of the work.

How to Wind a Butterfly

1. Place the end of the yarn across your left hand and wind the yarn around your thumb and small finger. Bring the yarn around your small finger and back across your hand and around your thumb again. Continue with this motion to make a figure eight with the yarn.

2. When you have wound as much yarn as you need, cut the yarn from the ball and wind the end around the center of the butterfly. Tuck in the end.

3. Remove the butterfly from your hand, and pull the yarn from the center. This is a miniature version of pulling yarn from the center of a skein.

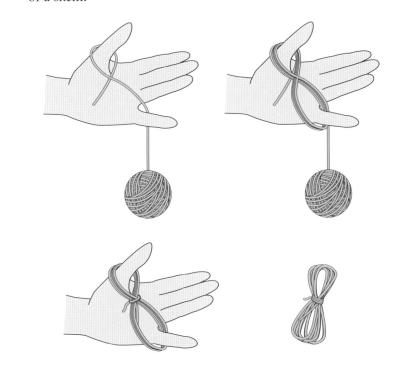

Afghan Stitch
(or Tunisian Simple Stitch)

The afghan stitch can be used to make many decorative accessories and clothing in addition to afghans. It's unique because it uses a special hook, known as an afghan hook, which is a longer-than-normal hook. This stitch uses more yarn, but the result is a very dense and warm fabric.

Afghan stitch or Tunisian simple stitch

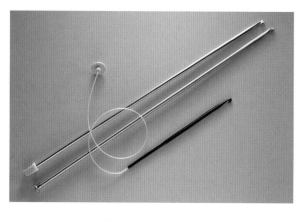

Afghan stitch hooks

The width of the work is determined by the length of the hook, so the projects are often made in strips and then joined together. The chained or beginning edge, and sometimes the bound-off edge, has a tendency to roll toward the right side and will require steaming or perhaps an edging to stop the problem. There are several variations to the afghan stitch, but we'll only discuss the basic pattern in this book.

The basic pattern comprises 2 rows that are always worked on the right side. The first row consists of placing loops for every stitch of the row on the hook—which is why it requires a special hook that is extra long—and the second row consists of binding off each stitch. The result is a square grid pattern, which is often embroidered over in a manner similar to counted cross-stitch.

TO WORK STARTING CHAIN AND FIRST 2 ROWS:

Make a chain for the exact number of stitches you need.

Row 1: Insert the hook into the top loop only of the second chain from the hook, yarn over hook, and pull through chain; keep that loop on the hook (2 loops on hook). Insert the hook into the chain, yarn over hook, and pull through a loop for each chain stitch across, keeping all loops on the hook. At the end of the row, you should have a loop on the hook for every chain. Do not turn work.

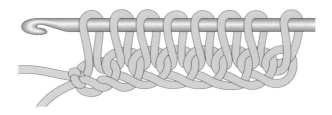

Row 2: With the right side still facing you, yarn over hook and pull through 1 loop. This counts as the turning chain for the second row.

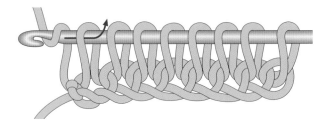

*Yarn over hook and pull through 2 loops. Repeat from * across the row until 1 loop remains.

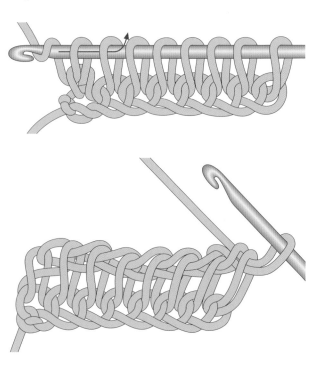

Work the remainder of the rows as follows:

TO WORK FORWARD ROW:

Insert the hook under the first vertical thread of a stitch (don't work into the vertical thread below the loop on your hook), yarn over hook and pull through a loop; keep it on the hook. Repeat across the row to the last vertical thread. Insert the hook under both vertical threads at the end, yarn over hook, and pull through a loop.

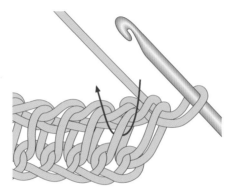

First stitch in forward row

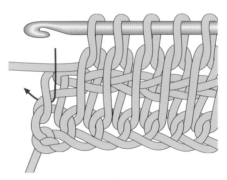

Last stitch in forward row

TO WORK RETURN ROW:

Repeat row 2 as given for the starting chain.

Repeat these 2 rows for the pattern stitch.

DECREASES

Worked on the forward row of the pattern stitch, decreases are made by working 2 stitches together. Decreases can be worked at the beginning or the end of the row.

Decreases shown in white

TO WORK:

Insert the hook under 2 vertical threads at the same time. Yarn over hook and pull through both vertical threads; keep the loop on the hook. This is worked in the same manner at either end of the row.

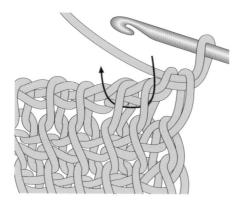

INCREASES

Worked on the forward row, increases are made by working an extra stitch before the first stitch or between 2 normal stitches.

Increases shown in white

TO WORK:

Insert the hook under the strand that lies behind the 2 horizontal threads that are between 2 vertical threads, yarn over hook, and pull through a loop, giving you an extra loop on the hook. This is worked in the same manner at either end of the row. On the next row, the extra loop is treated as a normal stitch.

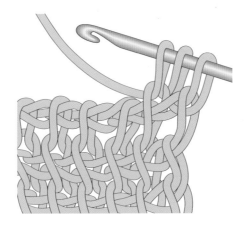

BINDING OFF

The most common ways of binding off in afghan stitch are working a row of slip stitch or a row of single crochet.

Bind off with slip stitch.

Bind off with single crochet.

TO BIND OFF WITH SLIP STITCH:

At the beginning of a forward row, *insert the hook under the first vertical thread of a stitch as you normally would, yarn over hook, and pull through both loops on the hook (1 loop remains on hook). Repeat from * across to last vertical thread. Insert the hook into both vertical threads at the end, yarn over hook, and pull through both loops on the hook. Fasten off.

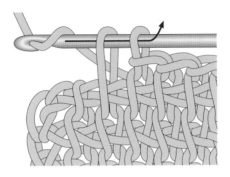

TO BIND OFF WITH SINGLE CROCHET:

At the beginning of a forward row, *insert the hook under the first vertical thread of a stitch as you normally would, yarn over hook and pull through a loop. Then yarn over hook and pull through both loops (1 loop remains on hook). Repeat from * across to last vertical thread. Insert the hook into both vertical threads at the end, yarn over hook and pull through a loop, yarn over hook and pull through both loops. Fasten off.

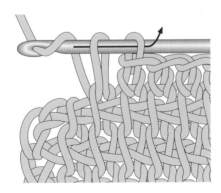

Blocking and Storage

In general, I don't do a lot of blocking. If the crochet is even and the tension is correct, the pieces should need very little blocking. Exceptions might be seams that need some taming or corners that are rolling after the garment is completed. Depending on the yarn and the project's intended use, the blocking process can be vigorous with starch for a doily or quite gentle for silk. In general, a little water and steam works for almost everything. *Never, under any circumstance, let the iron touch anything you're blocking.* The weight of the iron could smash the stitches and ruin the texture forever. You can also use any of the blocking methods to freshen a garment that has been worn but doesn't need washing.

The following are some general rules for blocking specific fibers.

+ **Synthetic Fibers:** Acrylic, polyester, and nylon don't usually need blocking. To clean, wash and dry flat. You can place a damp cloth on the garment, if necessary, to keep it flat.

+ **Animal Fibers:** Angora, alpaca, cashmere, mohair, and wool can be hand washed, so you can block them with a little steam or dampen them completely and allow them to dry. Use as little friction as possible to prevent felting. If steaming, be careful with angora and mohair; you don't want to destroy the "furriness."

+ **Plant Fibers:** Cotton, rayon, linen, and silk require little blocking. If necessary, all can be dampened and left to dry. Cotton will stretch when damp, but it will return to size when placed in the dryer or placed under heat.

Below are common washing and dry-cleaning symbols found on most yarn labels or purchased garment labels.

Washing		Pressing	
⊠	Do not wash	⊠	Do not iron
⊔	Hand wash in warm water	⌁	Cool iron
⌐30°⌐	Hand wash at stated temperature	⌁	Warm iron
⊡ ⊡	Machine wash	⌁	Hot iron
⊠	Do not tumble dry		
○	Tumble drying OK	**Dry-Cleaning Symbols**	
⊟	Dry flat		
⊠	No bleach	○	Dry clean
⚠	Chlorine bleach OK		

DAMP BLOCKING

Test the following damp-blocking method on your swatch before using it on a garment.

+ Immerse the garment in water, or spray it with water until it's damp.

+ Using a flat surface larger than the garment, lay your garment out flat and shape to the measurements. If necessary, pin along the edges with stainless-steel T-pins.

+ Place a heavy, cotton bath towel over the garment until dry. Replace the damp towel with a dry one as needed.

+ Keep the garment in a warm, dry place out of the sunlight until dry.

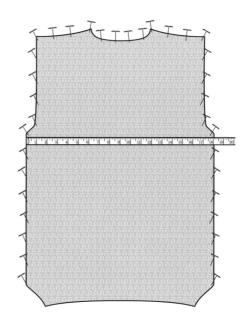

STEAM BLOCKING

Test the following steam-blocking method on your swatch before using it on a garment.

+ Use this method for an entire garment, just for seams, or to tame points of collars or front edges.

+ Using a flat surface larger than the garment, lay your garment out flat and shape to the measurements. If necessary, pin along the edges with stainless-steel T-pins.

+ The garment can be slightly damp, or instead, dampen the pressing cloth or towel. Cover the garment with the pressing cloth or towel.

+ Hold the iron above the work, gently touching the pressing cloth if necessary. Don't move the iron as though you were "ironing." Pick the iron up and move it to the next spot.

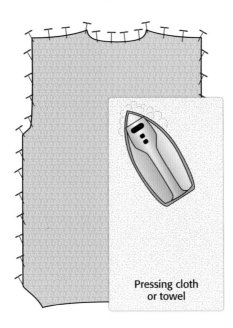

Pressing cloth
or towel

STORAGE

+ Always be sure that whatever you're storing is clean and dry before you put it away.

+ Never hang a crocheted garment. Fold it with as few folds as possible. Flat is perfect!

+ If you hand wash the garment, be sure it can be dried in a reasonable time so that it doesn't begin to smell musty.

+ Store garments or afghans in plastic boxes to keep moths and other bugs from harming them. Be careful if you have high humidity so that the boxes don't get moisture inside.

+ Be sure to store boxes in a cool place away from any dampness. Extreme conditions can have an effect on yarn.

+ These rules also apply to storing yarn.

+ For starched doilies and tablecloths in fine thread, roll them on tubes with tissue paper so that they don't form fold lines.

Index

About the Author

In 1987, while still working as a registered nurse, Nancie Wiseman opened a yarn shop called Nancie Knits in Sacramento, California. This started Nancie on a dynamic career as a popular designer of, and nationally known teacher of, knitted and crocheted garments. She has designed patterns for top yarn companies, including Cascade Yarns, Prism, Lorna's Laces, Rainbow Mills, and Trendsetter Yarns. Her articles and designs have been published in *Interweave Knits, Knit 'n Style, Knitter's Magazine,* and *Piecework.* Nancie was also a consultant and designer for a "Knitting 101" article in *Martha Stewart Living,* and contributed to the DVD *The Art of Knitting.* She's appeared on the DIY Network's *Jewelry Making Show* on cable television and the *Shay Pendray Needlearts Studio* on PBS. In 1995, Nancie started the production company Wisewater Productions, and it has produced seven bestselling videos.

Nancie's books include *Knitted Shawls, Stoles, and Scarves* (Martingale & Company, 2001), *The Knitter's Book of Finishing Techniques* (Martingale & Company, 2002), *Classic Knitted Vests* (Martingale & Company, 2003), and *Classic Crocheted Vests* (Martingale & Company, 2004).

Nancie lives on Whidbey Island, Washington, in the quaint town of Coupeville with her husband, Bill Attwater, and their dogs, Amber, a golden retriever, and Pumpkin, a Yorkie.

Knitting and Crochet Titles

Martingale® & COMPANY

America's Best-Loved Craft & Hobby Books®
America's Best-Loved Knitting Books®

CROCHET

Classic Crocheted Vests

Crochet from the Heart *NEW!*

Crochet for Babies and Toddlers

Crochet for Tots

Crocheted Aran Sweaters

Crocheted Lace

Crocheted Socks!

Crocheted Sweaters

First Crochet *NEW!*

Fun and Funky Crochet *NEW!*

The Little Box of Crocheted Hats and Scarves

More Crocheted Aran Sweaters *NEW!*

Today's Crochet

Our books are available at bookstores and your favorite craft, fabric, and yarn retailers. If you don't see the title you're looking for, visit us at www.martingale-pub.com or contact us at:

1-800-426-3126

International:
1-425-483-3313

Fax: 1-425-486-7596

Email: info@martingale-pub.com

KNITTING

200 Knitted Blocks

365 Knitting Stitches a Year: Perpetual Calendar

Basically Brilliant Knits

Beyond Wool

Big Knitting *NEW!*

Classic Knitted Vests

Comforts of Home

Dazzling Knits

Fair Isle Sweaters Simplified

First Knits

Garden Stroll, A

Handknit Style

Knit It Now!

Knits for Children and Their Teddies

Knits from the Heart

Knitted Shawls, Stoles, and Scarves

Knitted Throws and More for the Simply Beautiful Home

The Knitter's Book of Finishing Techniques

A Knitter's Template

Knitting with Hand-Dyed Yarns

Knitting with Novelty Yarns

Lavish Lace

The Little Box of Knitted Ponchos and Wraps *NEW!*

The Little Box of Knitted Throws *NEW!*

The Little Box of Scarves

The Little Box of Scarves II

The Little Box of Sweaters

More Paintbox Knits

Perfectly Brilliant Knits *NEW!*

The Pleasures of Knitting

Pursenalities

Rainbow Knits for Kids

Sarah Dallas Knitting

Saturday Sweaters *NEW!*

Sensational Knitted Socks *NEW!*

Simply Beautiful Sweaters

Simply Beautiful Sweaters for Men

Style at Large

A Treasury of Rowan Knits

The Ultimate Knitted Tee

The Ultimate Knitter's Guide

06/05